Perth Theatre at Horsecross Arts and Morna Young present

LOST at SEA

By Morna Young

T0348012

WRITER'S NOTE

Every story begins with an inciting incident, a moment when the balance is tipped, an event or turning point that sets everything into motion. My moment was an accident. A fishing accident on 10th April 1989. For on that day, my dad – Daniel 'Donnie' Young – was lost at sea. His body was never recovered.

Children don't understand death. Not really. The concept of time is a bit of an anomaly; the idea of forever and ever is just too much to comprehend. There's only yesterday, today, tomorrow and perhaps the day after that. Writing "Lost at Sea" was my chance, many years later, to grieve. I tore through the past to make sense of the present. I collected memory fragments and stories about my dad to sketch an outline of who he was.

My story is not unusual in fishing communities. Men and boats from all around the coast have been lost, every village scarred by these losses. We're forever bound by the salt in our blood. Writing this play was my opportunity to pay tribute. I wanted to create a fictional story but to use 'real voices' within it, and I am honoured that so many people put their trust in me. Though the story itself is imagined and infused with artistic licence, the truth behind it is not. These voices exist all around us.

Early in my research, a fisherman sent me the following email:

"The 'glory years' of the fishing. 75-95. Boats from the villages started working further afield, catching vast amounts of fish and earning, at that time, fantastic money. They were crazy days with big money, big cars, bigger houses, long hours, short times at home. Work hard, live hard. But there was now what I see to be deemed as an acceptable risk that only became unacceptable when you were directly involved. It was like Russian roulette as to who lived and who died. I lost some friends... which could have been me if I took different choices. Not good choices, just lucky ones. Every village lost a boat or two with all crew over this period plus the individuals lost overboard. It was like a war – men go away but not all come back and this was accepted as part of the price to pay for earning the money and keeping the villages alive."

This email set the story of the play in motion. It showed the personal intertwining with the political, the economics and the culture. This voice is one of many I have tried to capture within the play. I cannot express my gratitude enough to those who shared their stories. I thank them for their bravery and kindness.

Personal narratives don't end with a revelation and a resolution. This play has a finale but there is no end to the grief experienced by coastal communities. I once heard someone on the radio say *'when you die, you become the subject of stories'* and the sentiment has stayed with me. Those we have lost live on through the stories we share. I hope, in some small way, that this work helps honour their memory.

Morna Young, 2019.

ACKNOWLEDGEMENTS

This production of *Lost at Sea* is the result of many great people investing their time, energy and commitment. The words "I believe in you" are more valuable than any currency.

To the legendary Muriel Romanes for seeing possibility. To Mike Griffiths for sticking by me during the tough times. To Tina McGeever for giving me a home when I needed one the most. To Ian Brown for the unwavering belief and encouragement. To Alex Fthenakis for being my rock. To Kate Gillies for helping me understand who I was. To Lu Kemp, Anna Beedham and all at Perth Theatre for taking a chance. To all at Stellar Quines, Out of the Darkness Theatre Company and the Moray Council. To Sandy Thomson and all at Poorboy. To Karen Dick and all at Creative Scotland. To Playwrights' Studio, Scotland and Peter Arnott for calling me 'a playwright'. To Neil McPherson and all at the Finborough. To the casts of both the Lossiemouth and Finborough readings. To Angie, Lucy, David, Jenny, Kim, Cat, Martin / Ken, Stuart, Paula, Rachael, Serena, Sandy, Alan, Fiona, Hilda, Laurie, Holly... for the tears, the beers and fighting fears. To Shane Strachan for haudin ma haun. To Selwyn, Enid, Buff, Bobo, Juice, Charles, Grant, Daniel, Iain, Janet and Ivan. To Chris for truth and true heroism. To Rev Ray Hall and all at the Fishermen's Mission. To Richard Lochhead, MSP. To the Buckie Heritage Centre, Scottish Fisheries Museum, Edinburgh University and the School of Scottish Studies. To Derek and the fishermen who let me join their crew and those at the Burghead and Hopeman sheddies. To Ken Alexander and Andrew Comrie. To Gerry McAllister and all at the Peterhead Port Authority. To Eden Court, the Northern Scot, Lossiemouth Town Hall, Commercial Hotel, Stotfield Hotel, Right Lines and Wildbird. To Dani Rae, Liz Carruthers, Susannah Armitage, Lynda Radley, Paddy Cuneen, Clare Duffy, Julie Ellen and Lesley Hart. To Duncan Hendry, Nick Fearne, Colin Marr, Iain Copeland, Jane Litster, George Gunn, John Cairns, Jacqui Taylor, Lindsay Brown and Susan Macalister Hall. To Georgina Young and Melissa MacDonald. To Jane Dolby and The Fishwives. To the Moray residents – particularly those from Burghead, Hopeman, Lossie and Buckie – who contributed their stories, photographs, films and time. To my agent Michael Eliot–Finch and all at Brennan Artists. To Corey Arnold. To our extraordinary cast and creative team for their dedication and talent. To those I have forgotten – I apologise and thank you.

I also want to thank my family for supporting my journey into the unknown; Stella, Anne, Doug, Jimmy, Jen, Madje, Dougie and beyond. For your trust, faith, honesty, belief – and for always having a large dram at the ready.

DIRECTOR'S NOTE

Lost at Sea is an ambitious play. I admire and love it for that. It has a large cast, it demands movement and sound. It has live music and rich language celebrating the Doric language of North East Scotland. It plays with theatrical form. We move backwards and forwards in time. There are ghosts. There is a chorus.

Lost at Sea is about many things. The power of the sea, its unpredictability and its indifference to humankind. It's about the resoluteness of fisherfolk and the sheer hard graft and danger they face every day. It's a play about family and rivalry. It's about relationships and betrayal – unspoken love and the ties that bind.

The play is about an unexplained death. It is Shona's story, her attempt to open up the past so she can face her future. A sense of mortality and loss pervades the landscape – the ghosts of those lost at sea. It is a search for meaning of the lives taken; the enduring constancy of love, land and sea. The ghosts that haunt us.

Ian Brown, 2019.

LOST AT SEA

Lost at Sea premiered on 27 April 2019 at Perth Theatre. The play ran at this venue for two weeks before touring across Scotland to Dundee Rep Theatre; His Majesty's Theatre, Aberdeen; The Beacon Arts Centre, Greenock; Eden Court, Inverness; Kings Theatre, Edinburgh and Easterbrook Hall, Dumfries as part of the D&G Arts Festival.

Cast

Shona	Sophia McLean
Skipper	Tam Dean Burn
Mate/Musician	Thoren Ferguson
Billy	Gerry Mulgrew
Meg	Jennifer Black
Kevin	Andy Clark
Kath	Helen McAlpine
Jock	Ali Craig
Eve	Kim Gerard

Creative Team

Writer	Morna Young
Director	Ian Brown
Composer and Sound Design	Pippa Murphy
Designer	Karen Tennent
Lighting	Katharine Williams
Movement Director	Jim Manganello
Associate Director	Rosa Duncan
Voice and Dialect	Ros Steen

The first public rehearsed reading of *Lost at Sea* took place on 1 March 2013 in Lossiemouth Town Hall. It was presented as a co-production between Morna Young, Stellar Quines Theatre Company, Out of the Darkness Theatre Company and the Moray Council. Award winning Muriel Romanes directed the play and Peter Arnott dramaturged the performance. The cast were as follows:

Shona	Melissa Paterson
The Man	Tam Dean Burn
Billy	Kern Falconer
Meg	Carol Ann Crawford
Kevin	Cameron Mowat
Kath	Emilie Patry
Jock	Ross Allan
Eve	Lesley Hart
Ensemble	Estrid Barton
Ensemble	David Rankine

A secondary reading took place as part of The Finborough Theatre's Vibrant Festival 2015, directed by Liz Carruthers. The cast were as follows:

Shona	Isobella Hubbard
The Man	Stuart Bowman
Billy	David McKail
Meg	Lindy Whiteford
Kevin	Adam McNamara
Kath	Patricia Kavanagh
Jock	Ross F Sutherland
Eve	Sharon Young
Ensemble	Cara Ballingall
Ensemble	Ben Clifford

Produced by

Perth Theatre at Horsecross Arts, Scotland

Artistic Director	Lu Kemp
Producer	Anna Beedham
Production Manager	Gavin Johnston
Company Stage Manager	Sandra Grieve
Production Stage Manager	Michael Heasman
Deputy Stage Manager	Jessica Ward
Assistant Stage Manager	Dayna Cumming
Head of Stage	David Freeburn
Stage Carpenter	Zach Allen
Workshop Assistant	Greg Powrie
Head of Lighting	Karin Anderson
Senior Lighting Technician	Fee Dalgleish
Head of Sound	Ritchie Young
Seasonal Sound	Gabe Kemp
Head of Costume	Louise Robertson
Costume Assistant	Pat Jastrzebska
Scenic Artist	Martha Steed

Thanks to our partners and funders

PERTH & KINROSS COUNCIL

CREATIVE SCOTLAND · ALBA | CHRUTHACHAIL

The Gannochy Trust

Cover image by Corey Arnold.

Cast

Jennifer Black Meg
Jennifer's recent theatre credits include: *Arctic Oil; One Good Beating; Kill The Old Torture Their Young; House Among the Stars* and *The Bench* (Traverse); *The Iliad, Tartuffe, Six Black Candles, A Streetcar Named Desire, Peter Pan, Macbeth, An Experienced Woman Gives Advice, Dead Funny, On Golden Pond* and *Blithe Spirit* (Lyceum); *The Cone Gatherers* (Aberdeen Performing Arts); *Safe Place, 10,000 Metres Deep* and *Leather Bound* (Òran Mór); *A Taste of Honey* (TAG Theatre); *Three Thousand Troubled Threads* and *The Memory of Water* (both Stellar Quines TC); *The Bans* (Theatre Babel); *Falling* and *Buried Treasure* (Bush Theatre); *Too Late for Logic* (King's Theatre); *Stiff – The Musical* (Diva Productions) and *Lavotchikin, Ashes to Ashes, The Trick is to Keep Breathing, Good* and *The Baby* (Tron) and *Sacred Hearts* (Communicado TC).

Jennifer's film and television credits include: *Doctors, River City, Holby City, Half Moon Investigations, Still Game, Why do They Call It Good Friday, A View of Things* and *Ploughman's* (all BBC); *Rebus* (SMG); *Tinsel Town, Taggart, Out in the Open* and *Ugly Sisters* (all, STV); *I Saw You* (Channel 4); *The Bill* (Thames Television); *Local Hero* (Goldcrest Films) and *Heavenly Pursuits* (Skebo Films).

Her radio credits include: *Under the Skin, Week Ending* and *The Trick is to Keep Breathing* (all BBC Radio 4).

Andy Clark Kevin
Originally from Blairgowrie, Andy studied at Dundee College and RSAMD (now RCS). Recent theatre credits include: *Tartuffe* (Oran Mor); *A Christmas Carol* (Citizens); *The Buke of the Howlat* (Findhorn Bay Arts); *Antony & Cleopatra, Edward II* (Bard in the Botanics); *The Deep* (IOft Tall); *Stand By* (Utter); *Music Is Torture* (Tromolo/Tron); *The Winter's Tale* (Lyceum).

Other theatre includes *A Steady Rain* (Theatre Jezebel/Tron); *Dance of Death* (Candice Edmunds/Citizens); *Lanark* (Citizens/Lyceum/EIF); *Little Sure Shot* (West Yorkshire Playhouse/The Egg); *Gastronauts* (Royal Court); *I'm With the Band* (Traverse); *Mince, The Duchess of Malfi, The Seagull* (Dundee Rep); *Lampedusa,*

The Libertine, Hamlet, Othello, Peter Pan, Vernon God Little and *A Handful of Dust* (Citizens Theatre). Radio includes *Killing Kate, Boswell At Large, Big Sky, Five of Spades, Rebus* (BBC Radio 4).

Television and film credits include: *The Da Vinci Code* (Rose Line) *River City, Bob Servant* (BBC Scotland); *Rebus, Taggart* (STV); *Rubenesque* (Kudos).

Andy is delighted to be back at the wonderfully renovated Perth Theatre having first appeared on stage here over 30 years ago as a pirate in a concert for the Boys' Brigade.

Ali Craig Jock

Ali trained at the Mountview Academy of Theatre Arts, London. His theatre credits include: *The James Plays* (National Theatre); *The 306, The Making of Us, Macbeth, Beautiful Burnout* (Frantic Assembly) and *Black Watch* (National Theatre Scotland); *Into That Darkness* (Citizens Theatre); *The BFG, Hecuba, Victoria* (Dundee Rep Theatre); *The Secret Garden* (Footlights Productions); *Hamlet* (Greenwich Theatre) and *Waterproof* (Òran Mór).

Ali's television credits include: *Armchair Detectives, Trust Me, Outlander, Shetland, River, The Monarch of the Glen, Sea of Souls* and *Black Watch*.

His film credits include: Gregor Barclays and Colin Bell's *Ribbons,* Stuart Urban's *May I Kill U?,* Graham Eatough's *The Making of Us,* Steve Barker's *Outpost: Black Sun,* Karl Golden's *Weekender* and *Pelican Blood,* and John L'Ecuyer's *The Good Times Are Killing Me.* Short film credits include: *And Repeat* (Richard Poet).

On radio his credits include: *Keeping Mum, Topaz, McLevy, Immaculate* and *Black Watch* for BBC Radio.

Tam Dean Burn Skipper

Tam began his acting career at Perth Theatre as acting assistant stage manager for the season 1980-81 under Joan Knight and Patrick Sandford. His one appearance in Perth since then was in Rapture's *The Collection* in 2013, the same year he took part in the first rehearsed reading of *Lost at Sea* in Lossiemouth.

He previously worked with director Ian Brown in *Hardie and Baird:*

The Last Days, Stones and Ashes (Traverse Theatre) and Irvine Welsh's *You'll Have Had Your Hole* (West Yorkshire Playhouse and London Astoria). Tam has appeared in many films, starting with *Local Hero* in 1983 and most recently *Outlaw King*.

His television roles include several years as the gangster McCabe in *River City* and he will feature in the forthcoming BBC shows *The Victim* and *Trust Me 2*.

Following the *Lost at Sea* tour he travels to New York with the Scottish National Jazz Orchestra to perform Liz Lochhead's version of *Peter and the Wolf*.

Thoren Ferguson Mate/musician
Thoren is a Scottish actor, musician and composer. This year he can be seen in the principal role of David Fairbairn in the independent feature horror/thriller *Matriarch*.

In 2018 Thoren became the face of global whisky giant Johnnie Walker, making nine commercials for worldwide distribution. Thoren collaborated with film-maker/director Charlotte Wells on her 2018 Sundance selected and Grand Jury nominated short film *Blue Christmas*, playing the role of Johnny. He also featured in screen roles in the BBC TV series *Clique*, BBC iPlayer series *Logan High* and game drama *Armchair Detectives*. In 2018 he returned to his stage acting roots to tour Scotland in the male lead role of Arnaud in Eden Court Theatre's well-received play *The Return*.

Thoren leads the ceilidh band The Jacobites, founders of The Edinburgh Street Ceilidh. He composed *Armistice*, to commemorate the centenary of the signing of the Armistice. This was played by an international orchestra of 40 ensembles across the world.

Thoren has played as a soloist at events across the country; to HRH Princess Anne at the opening of Dreghorn commemorative wood, with the Scottish Fiddle Orchestra at concerts across the country, and he's also won fiddle competitions across Scotland. His published compositions are *Armistice, The Lads of Quintinshill, 1915, The Somme*, and *Wilfred Owen*. In 2018 he played at the graveside of Wilfred Owen as part of the official commemoration of the centenary of the poet's death.

Kim Gerard Eve

Kim has appeared on stage in *Sense* (Frozen Charlotte Theatre Company); *Peter Pan, The Man Who Had All The Luck, Mary Rose, Vanity Fair* and *Living Quarters* (Lyceum); *Call It Sleep* and *Elf Analysis* (Òran Mór); *Sunshine On Leith, Hansel and Gretel, Sweet Bird Of Youth* and *A Midsummer Night's Dream* (Dundee Rep) *Romeo and Juliet* (Shakespeare's Globe, Sam Wanamaker Festival).

Her radio credits include: *Words and Music Free Thinking Festival, Writing The Century, Solitary Bird, Care, Striptease, Mclevy* and *Legacy* (BBC). She also appeared in the short films *Stay Awake* (Bombito Productions) and *Harder* (Greenroom Films).

Helen McAlpine Kath

Helen trained at QMUC. Her theatre credits include: *The Last Bordello* (Fire Exit) *Sleeping Cutie, Chick Whittington, Weans in the Wood, The Little Mermaid, Aladdin, Peter Pan, The Happy Prince, Snow White of the Seven De'Wharffs, Jackie & The Beanstalk* (Macrobert); *Beowulf* (Tron/Home Place); *Peter Panto & The Incredible Stinkerbell, Cannibal Women of Mars, Aganeza Scrooge, The Tempest* (Tron Theatre); *Ice Cream Dreams, The Wizard of Oz, Cinderella* (Citizen's Theatre); *Rough Island, Whisky Galore, Singing Far into the Night, Swindle & Death* (Mull Theatre Company); *The Steamie* (Pitlochry Festival Theatre); *The Girl With Red Hair* (Lyceum/Bush); *Doris, Dolly & the Dressing Room Divas'* (Òran Mór /Gilded Balloon); *The Last Picture Show, We Can All Agree To Pretend This Never Happened* (Òran Mór).

Television and film credits include: *The Sopranos* (In A Big Country Films); *Trust Me* (Red Productions/BBC); *Rillington Place* (Bandit/BBC); *Shetland* (ITV); *Waterloo Road* (BBC); *Field of Blood* (Slate North/BBC); *Rab C Nesbitt, The Limmy Show* (The Comedy Unit); *Taggart* (SMG); *Intergalactic Kitchen, Stacey Stone* (CBBC).

Sophia McLean Shona

In 2017 Shona was nominated for Society of London Theatre's Laurence Olivier Bursary Award and was a 2018 finalist of The Spotlight Prize. She graduated from Drama Studio London in July 2018. Recent theatre credits include: *The Last Days of Mankind* (Leith Theatre); *Scribble* (Assembly Roxy) and *Theatre Uncut: The Power Plays* (Braw Fox Theatre) and for radio: *Macbeth* (Almost Tangible).

Gerry Mulgrew Billy

Gerry was awarded Best Male Performance at the CATS 2007, for his role as Old Peer in *Peer Gynt* (Dundee Rep and National Theatre of Scotland).

Gerry's extensive theatre credits include: *Ma, Pa and the Little Mouths* (Tron); *Krapp's Last Tape* (Tron/Blood of the Young); *Losing the Rag, The Last Dictator, The Above* and *Federer vs Murray* (Glasgow Òran Mór); *Ay! Carmela!* (Out of the Box); *My Name is Ben, The Visit* and *Ubu the King* (all Dundee Rep); *Peer Gynt* (Dundee Rep/ NTS); *Waiting for Godot* (Citizens Theatre); *Lanark* (Citizens Theatre/ Edinburgh International Festival); *Nova Scotia* and *Tree of Knowledge* (Traverse); *Ane Satyre of the Three Estates* (Staging for the Scottish Court).

Gerry is a founding member and the Artistic Director of Communicado Theatre Company, where his credits include: *The Government Inspector, The Memorandum, The Suicide, A Place with the Pigs, Cyrano de Bergerac, The Cone Gatherers, Mary Queen of Scots, Carmen, The Hunchback of Notre Dame* and *The House with the Green Shutters*.

Creative Team

Morna Young Writer

Morna is a playwright, actress and musician from a wee fishing village in the North East of Scotland. She was recipient of the 2017 Dr Gavin Wallace Fellowship (hosted by Creative Learning, Aberdeen City Council) where she explored the theme 'the Folk, the Language and the Landscape of the North East'. Other accolades include: the 'Tomorrow at Noon' award for female playwrights 2018 (Jermyn Street Theatre) and the New Playwrights Award 2014 (Playwrights' Studio, Scotland). She was playwright-in-residence for BATS Theatre and Toi Pōneke Arts Centre in Wellington, New Zealand in 2018 as part of an ongoing international exchange between Scotland and New Zealand (Playmarket and Playwrights' Studio, Scotland).

Lost at Sea was her first full-length play, written in 2012. Other plays include: *Aye, Elvis* ('A Play, A Pie and A Pint' and Gilded Balloon at Edinburgh Fringe); *The Buke of the Howlat* (Findhorn Bay Arts); *Smite* (Jermyn Street Theatre); *Netting* ('A Play, A Pie and A Pint' and Scotland-wide tour with Woodend Barn); *She of the Sea* (Paines Plough 'Come to Where I'm From' at the Lemon Tree); *B-Roads* (Play Pieces); *Never Land* (Eden Court) and two short plays for the National Theatre of Scotland's *Great Yes, No, Don't Know Show*.

Morna has performed extracts of her work at the Scottish Parliament, The European Author's Festival (Czech Republic, Slovakia, Poland); National Poetry Month (France) and Edinburgh International Book Festival. Morna primarily writes in Doric and is a proud Scots Language Ambassador (Education Scotland).

Full information at: www.mornayoung.com

Ian Brown Director

Lost at Sea marks a welcome return to Scotland by Ian Brown who was Artistic Director of The Traverse Theatre in Edinburgh for eight years. During that time, he directed and produced a wide range of new writing notably plays by Jo Clifford, Anne Marie Di Mambro, Chris Hannan, Sue Glover, David Greig and David Harrower. He introduced Brad Fraser's work to the UK and transferred *Love and Human Remains* and *Poor Super Man* to Hampstead Theatre.

Brown's production of *Moscow Stations* with Tom Courtenay transferred to The Garrick Theatre. He oversaw the successful move from The Grassmarket to Cambridge Street. During this time, he directed the original stage production of *Trainspotting*. His production of *Bondagers* by Sue Glover toured Scotland and played a season at London's Donmar Theatre. It was also part of the Toronto New Stages Festival.

Brown trained at Central School of Speech and Drama, became a drama teacher in a comprehensive school in Stoke Newington. He later ran the Cockpit Youth Theatre, commissioning new plays and large-scale musicals. After a spell as Philip Hedley's Associate Director at Theatre Royal, Stratford East, he was appointed Artistic Director of Tag Theatre Company at the Citizens' Theatre Glasgow. His production of Jo Clifford's *Great Expectations* toured to India, Iraq, Sri Lanka and Bangladesh.

After leaving Scotland Brown was behind an impressive series of freelance productions including two new plays for The Royal Shakespeare Company (Richard Nelson and David Greig). He then became Associate Director, and subsequently Artistic Director, of West Yorkshire Playhouse. Major productions included *Hamlet* with Christopher Eccleston, *Pretending to be Me* with Tom Courtenay (transferred to Comedy Theatre); *Twelfth Night* with Hattie Morahan, *Hay Fever* with Maggie Steed, *Waiting for Godot* with Jeffery Kissoon and Patrick Robinson and *King Lear* with Tim Pigott Smith.

Now based in London, Brown regularly directs and teaches at Lamda, Rose Bruford College and EI5 Acting School and Guildhall School. He recently directed two plays at Park Theatre – *Contact.com* by Michael Kingsbury and Bryony Lavery's *Frozen* for Blueprint Theatre Company. Last year he directed *Lonely Planet* by Steven Dietz at Trafalgar Studios.

Rosa Duncan Associate Director
(supported by the Federation of Scottish Theatre's Directors Bursary)

Rosa trained at the Lancaster Institute of Contemporary Arts. Her directing credits include: *Learning to Read Labels* (Horsecross Arts/ Women of the World Festival); *After Words* (Edinburgh International Science Festival Scratch); *Berlin* (the music video for Scarlett Randle) and *Shopping Hungover* (BBC Comedy Short Stuff).

As an Assistant Director, her credits include: *The View from Castle Rock* (Stellar Quines/Edinburgh International Book Festival); *The Lonesome West* (Tron Theatre); *Great Expectations* (Horsecross Arts/Dundee Rep Theatre); *The Glass Menagerie* (Dundee Rep Theatre).

Rosa is currently directing *Which Wires What* (Imaginate/The Weather Channel) which will showcase at the Edinburgh International Children's Festival.

Karen Tennent Designer
Karen is a graduate of Edinburgh College of Art. Her work has toured all over the UK and abroad from village halls to Sydney Opera House.

Recent designs include: *First Snow* (NTS/Theatre PAP Montreal); *We are All Just Little Creatures* (Curious Seed /Lung Ha / Lyra); *Lots and Not Lots* (NTS FutureProof); *Glory on Earth, The Iliad, Caucasian Chalk Circle* (Royal Lyceum) *Emma and Gill ,Eddie and the Slumber Sisters, The Voice Thief, Lifeboat* (Catherine Wheels); *Lost in Music ,Our Fathers* (Magnetic North) *Teenage Trilogy, Chalk About* (Curious Seed); *Crumbles Search for Christmas* (West Yorkshire Playhouse); *God of Carnage, This Wide Night* (Tron Theatre); *ThingammyBob, The Three Sisters* (Lung Ha).

Karen also co-directed *Sonata for a Man and a Boy* (Greg Sinclair) winner of CATS best Children's Theatre. She was also won CATS best design and was nominated for the New York Drama Desk Awards for Outstanding Design for *Hansel and Gretel* (Catherine Wheels).

Katharine Williams Lighting
Katharine Williams lives in Edinburgh and has recently designed lighting for *Hole* (with RashDash at the Royal Court); *Gagarin Way* (Dundee Rep); *Women in Power* (Nuffield, Southampton); *Status* (China Plate); *All of Me* (China Plate); *The Rivals* (Watermill); *The Department of Distractions and Partus* (Third Angel); *Flood – Part Four* (SlungLow); *Two Man Show and The Darkest Corners* (RashDash); *Instructions for Border Crossings, Going Viral* and *Error 404* (Daniel Bye); *Big Guns* (Yard Theatre); *Medea* (Bristol Old Vic); *An Injury* (Permanent Red); *Am I Dead Yet?* (Unlimited); *Ode To Leeds* (West Yorkshire Playhouse) and was lead artist on the *Love Letters to the Home Office* project as well as being the founder of Crew for Calais.

Pippa Murphy Composer and Sound Design
Pippa Murphy is an award-winning composer and sound designer who writes for theatre, dance, film, choirs and orchestras. She has written music for BBC 2, BBC Radio 4, BBC Radio 3, Scottish Opera, SCO, BBCSSO, Edinburgh's Hogmanay and numerous theatre companies including The Royal Lyceum Edinburgh, Dundee Rep, Birmingham Rep, Grid Iron, Stellar Quines, Rapture Theatre, Traverse Theatre, 7:84.

Her sound design for Karine Polwart's *Wind Resistance* in the Edinburgh International Festival won the CATS Awards for Best Music & Sound 2018. Their album *Pocket of Wind Resistance* was nominated for BBC Folk Album of the Year 2018. Her music to *POP-UP Duets* for Janis Claxton Dance has been awarded 5-star reviews and been on an extensive world tour.

Pippa was classically trained on piano, violin and percussion from an early age and completed her BMus, MA and PhD composition at The University of Birmingham. She lectures at Edinburgh University and was Artist in Residence at the Scottish Parliament (2014).

Jim Manganello Movement Director
Jim is a director, movement director and performer based in Glasgow. He recently founded physical theatre company Shotput with Lucy Ireland. Their first piece, *Ferguson and Barton* recently premiered at Platform. Directing credits: *Lucia di Lammermoor* (Fulham Opera); *The Mute Quire, String Up the Moon* and *The Judge* (Fratellanza); *War and Peace* (Viaduct, Chicago).

As movement director: *Aladdin* (Perth); *The Enchanted Bullets* (Blackheath Halls); *Elixir of Love* (Scottish Opera); *Medea* (Festival Sortileges, Belgium); *Full Metal Jacket* (auQuai, Belgium). Acting credits: *Charlie Blows a Bulb* (Fratellanza); *The Playboy of the Western World* (Michigan Classical Rep); *The Skating Rink* (Garsington Opera). Training: École Lassaâd, Brussels.

Ros Steen Voice and Dialect

Perth Theatre credits: *Richard III, Knives in Hens, And Then Come The Nightjars*.

Recent theatre credits: *Our Ladies of Perpetual Succour, The James Plays* (tour); *Glasgow Girls, Macbeth, Black Watch* (NTS); *Local Hero* (Lyceum and Old Vic); *Cockpit, Hedda Gabler, Bondagers* (Lyceum); *What Girls are Made of, Meet Me at Dawn, Ciara* (Traverse); *Travels with my Aunt, True West* (Citizens' Theatre); *Hamlet, Romeo and Juliet* (Leeds Playhouse); *All My Sons, Death of a Salesman, The Cheviot, The Stag and the Black, Black Oil* (Dundee Rep); *Cyrano de Bergerac* (Northern Stage/Royal and Derngate).

Television, film and radio credits include: *Limbo* (GMac films); *Monarch of the Glen, 2,000 Acres of Sky* (TV)

Ros is Emeritus Professor of Voice and Editor of *Growing Voices*.

PERTH THEATRE

Perth Theatre reopened its doors to the public on Monday 13 November 2017 after its £16.6m transformation.

Perth Theatre has a long history of artistic innovation and excellence having been at the heart of cultural life in Perth for over a century. The transformation of the theatre has restored and redeveloped one of Scotland's oldest and best loved theatres for generations to come. The B listed Edwardian auditorium has been restored to its former glory and a new 200 seat studio theatre – the Joan Knight Studio – has been created. The newly transformed venue has increased workshop spaces for creative learning and community projects, including the thriving Perth Youth Theatre, as well as improved access and facilities for audiences and visitors.

As well as creating and touring its own productions, Perth Theatre collaborates with theatre companies and visiting artists to bring the best of local, national and international work to its stages.

Perth Theatre and sister venue Perth Concert Hall are managed by creative organisation and registered Scottish charity Horsecross Arts.

Horsecross Arts Board
Magnus Linklater CBE, Chair
Jason Elles, Vice Chair
Cllr Harry Coates
Alan Strachan
Anna Stapleton
Cllr John Rebbeck
Charles Kinnoull
Georgina Bullough
Cllr Willie Robertson
Stephanie Fraser
Jeannine McVean

Mike Griffiths, Chief Executive, Horsecross Arts

Our Supporters
The Green Room

Thank you to all the supporters who help to ensure a bright future for Perth Theatre. Big or small your gifts make a real difference.

Mrs Bowman, Barrie and Janey Lambie, Sir Ian Lowson BT, Iain G. Mitchell QC, Elaine Mccleary, Maureen Sturrock & Bob Turner, James Watt and all those who wish to remain anonymous.

www.horsecross.co.uk

LOST AT SEA

Morna Young

LOST AT SEA

OBERON BOOKS
LONDON

WWW.OBERONBOOKS.COM

First published in 2019 by Oberon Books Ltd
521 Caledonian Road, London N7 9RH
Tel: +44 (0) 20 7607 3637 / Fax: +44 (0) 20 7607 3629
e-mail: info@oberonbooks.com
www.oberonbooks.com

PB ISBN: 9781786827555
E ISBN: 9781786827531

Cover photo: Corey Arnold

Visit www.oberonbooks.com to read more about all our books and to buy them. You
will also find features, author interviews and news of any author events, and you can
sign up for e-newsletters so that you're always first to hear about our new releases.

Printed on FSC accredited paper

10 9 8 7 6 5 4 3 2 1

Dedicated to Donnie Young,
lost from the "Ardent II", 10th April 1989.

Lost at Sea is a personal tribute
to the fishing communities of Scotland.

The fishermen know that the sea is dangerous and the storm terrible, but they have never found these dangers sufficient reason for remaining ashore.
Vincent Van Gogh

As if the Sea should part
And show a further Sea –
And that – a further – and the Three
But a presumption be –

Of Periods of Seas –
Unvisited of Shores –
Themselves the Verge of Seas to be –
Eternity – is Those –
Emily Dickinson

Characters

SHONA

SKIPPER

MATE / MUSICIAN (VOICE 1)

BILLY (VOICE 2)

MEG (VOICE 5)

KEVIN (VOICE 3)

KATH (VOICE 6)

JOCK (VOICE 4)

EVE (VOICE 7)

FOR INFORMATION

All CHORUS parts are played by the company, led by the SKIPPER and MATE. These characters transcend all worlds. Strong characterisation is necessary to maintain clarity and pace throughout.

Choral lines allocated by voice number are optional and can be altered to suit the company / staging.

An additional FEMALE ENSEMBLE / MUSICIAN (VOICE 8) can be added to the core company. Similarly, additional musicians may help build the choral world.

LOST AT SEA spans forty years which involves all actors – minus the SKIPPER, SHONA, BILLY and JOCK – aging significantly throughout.

ACCENTS

SKIPPER, BILLY, MEG, JOCK, KEVIN and KATH should speak a strong colloquial version of Doric (Northeast Scots).

EVE is an 'incomer' to the village so can speak a softer version of Northeast Scots, though her accent may develop during the show. SHONA's accent can also be softer due to her time living away from the village.

LANGUAGE

LOST AT SEA features verbatim text from interviews with fishermen, their families and the local communities of the Northeast of Scotland. These interviews were conducted throughout 2011 and 2012. These 'real voices' have been woven into a fictional central story.

The transcribed verbatim text features several language inconsistencies due to regional speech differences. For example, a distinctive Doric trait like 'fit' is more commonly pronounced as 'whit' in Moray. Individual villages have their own speech variations and this is entirely changeable from place to place. Thus, the choral sections feature a range of language contradictions. However, SKIPPER's language embraces more 'traditional' Doric traits, particularly use of words like 'fit' and 'fa'.

This 'real speech' is echoed in dialogue throughout the play with characters saying the same word in multiple ways, for example, using 'to' and 'tae' in the same sentence.

PUNCTUATION

/ Slashes indicate overlapping dialogue.

– Dashes indicate a line that's cut off and / or a hesitation.

… Ellipses indicate the trailing off of a thought / searching for the right word / a suspension point.

Dialogue in brackets ( ) indicates that the audience doesn't necessarily hear the line.

SETTING

An unnamed fishing village on the Moray coast in the Northeast of Scotland.

The set should remain sparse and non-naturalistic. Music and movement are at the heart of the storytelling. The locations and 'moments in time' can be shown through space, objects and lighting. Memory is unreliable; perhaps this could be reflected somehow.

STAGE DIRECTIONS

Stage directions are suggestions only and the scene transitions are open to interpretation. Enjoy discovering the space between.

THE TRIBUTE

The 'in tribute' list of names are fishermen and boats lost from Moray during the timeframe of the play (1970 to 2012). This is not an exclusive list and has been pieced together from a range of resources. Any inaccuracies are solely the responsibility of the author.

*This text went to press before the end of rehearsals
so may differ slightly from the play as performed.*

ACT 1

SCENE 1

A darkened stage.

A single spotlight shows a sparse table and two chairs. KEVIN sits in one, arms folded. SHONA sits opposite.

She is flustered. She struggles to take off her jacket then rakes through her bag pulling out a notebook, pens and a diary. Finally, she retrieves a dictaphone which she places squarely on the table. She presses the record button.

A breath.

SHONA   Okay.

    A beat.

KEVIN   Ye'r a journalist.

SHONA   I was.

KEVIN   Is this gan tae be in the paper?

SHONA   This? About my dad?

                   No. This is for me.

KEVIN   Why the dictaphone?

SHONA   To remember.

    A beat.

KEVIN   Whit do ye want from me?

SHONA   The truth.

A sudden change of atmosphere, the stage engulfed by the sound and sight of the sea.

We see an abandoned wooden boat with SKIPPER perched on the side; a fisher, ragged and worn. Behind are the CHORUS; the voice of the community, of the ocean, of the dead.

ALL   Ye dream o the sea
                 the dark murky watter,
                 Ye long tae be free
                 fae the sound o time.
                 Ye'r tangled an trapped
                 in a tentacled bind,
                 Death is the shadow
                 drownin yer mind.

SKIPPER addresses the CHORUS whilst pointing at SHONA.

SKIPPER   She hears yer voices at nicht.

The VOICES echo.

VOICES   1. Ye'll niver find the truth.

                 2. Ye'r wastin yer time.

                 6. Tis a wild place oot in the dark watters.

                 3. Fit happens at the sea, stays at the sea.

                 4. She's lookin fer *answers.*

                 5. Trawlin. That's whit she's dein.

                 1. Stirrin it up.

                 7. Stickin her nose in.

ALL   We should be left in peace.

The CHORUS turn away. SHONA is upset.

SKIPPER   Look fit ye'v deen!

                 Salt tears –
                 Teeny wee drappies.

Harmless.

Salt watter –
An ocean.
Deadliest force on Earth.

D'ye ken, I niver really understood why
they caad it 'the Earth'. Maste o it's watter
efter aa.

(Sung.) Oh the sea, the sea,
A fishing life, sae free.
I robbed fae the ocean
And noo she's taken me!

C'mon quine… man versus the ocean. Fa
wis gan tae win that ane?

VOICES   1. Ye'r haverin, lass.

5. Send a wee lamby tae the slaughter, it's
nae gan tae come back noo, is it?

4. Fit chance did *we* hae?

The sea grows louder; thrashing, crashing, lashing. The wind swells.
Rain, thunder. A storm is brewing.

As SKIPPER leads the CHORUS, the voices whisper and echo like
the wind.

SKIPPER   The beastie braks banes; smashin, crashin,
lashin.
She'll pound ye, astound ye, ground ye tae a
fragment –
Crack, fracture, splinter –
crushin, pulverisin, shatterin yer existence,
slammin yer soul.

VOICES   2. … it's a dangerous animal, ken?

	4. Flat calm aey day an batterin ye stupit the next.
SKIPPER	Och, we used tae tame her, we did – Pray tae her, slave fer her, whistle her some wind, worship the waves an belittle the spirits o the land.
VOICES	6. You grow up in a fishin community, ye go tae the fishin.
	1. There's nae choice.
	2. I wisna feart when I wis younger. But as ye get auler… the fear…
	3. Never turn yer back. Niver rest.
SKIPPER	We aa needed the sea, didn't we? We took. She took. An eye for an eye, a man for a shoal.
VOICES	1. I went for the money. Same as aabody else.
	7. The stink o fish – the stink o money.
SKIPPER	And then – ye raped her.
VOICES	5. Too many chances. Too many close calls.
	4. Dodgin the weather for days an days.
	3. Plenty scares. Oh, ye'r thinkin, I'm nae gan tae get ower the top o this ane.
ALL	The strongest force in the world.
SKIPPER	Butcherin, maimin, torturin.

VOICES	2. They only found oot aboot rogue waves nae that long ago. Waves aboot 30 metres high.
	4. We'd seen thon things fer years.
	6. Caad them lumps o water.
	1. Christ, there's a lump comin here!
	3. Then –
ALL	SMASH.
SKIPPER	Ripped through her wi massive tanks and an industrial sized fleet.
VOICES	2. It wisna much o a life. But ye were prepared for it.
	3. You werena a man if ye werena dein it.
	1. Work hard, live hard.
	4. And if ye died…
	3. That was accepted.
	4. …aye… but if ye died…
SKIPPER	There will be a toll of lives.
	(To SHONA.) Is this the story ye'r after? Is this fit ye want tae hear?
	The untold war o man versus the elements. The tale o the fishermen fightin the ocean. Ye'v stirred the watters, opened the dam. There'll be a hearty tempest the nicht.

The storm hits; thunder and a flash of lightning.

SCENE 2

SKIPPER summons the CHORUS.

SKIPPER   1975. The year the Grateful wis lost. Throw her in at the deep end.

VOICE   2. Haul!

SKIPPER   Fa wis tae blame?

VOICE   2. Haul again, boys! Nearly there!

SKIPPER   Wis it the weather? The skipper? Fate?

VOICES   7. See, the fact is, there's nobody tae tell, naebody tae say *'this is the reason we didna get off'*. But that's whit goes through yer heid, whit you sit an think – how did they nae get off?

            1. Aa the boats in the area, we aa kent ane anither. The mayday screamed an we arrived tae –

            4. Nothin.

A beat.

            2. We wis oot searchin, pickin up bits o wid.

            1. We picked up a life jacket and a bit o the hold, aye, the registration number on it.

            2. A deck fill, a side deck fill o bits. Ken, ye wis lookin fer –

            1. Bodies.

            2. We wis lookin but we wisna. *I* wisna wantin tae find any.

            3. Ken, it wis aa yer freens ye wis lookin for.

18

4. Then a boat nae far from where we were…

2. They'd found somebody.

A moment.

1. I'd been standin on the pier on the Sunday night, speakin tae him… Moosey they caad him. Mickey McKenzie. He wis seventeen. And I wis sixteen.

4. The Pioneer picked somebody up. She says, 'we've picked up a young lad'. So we pulls alongside, nae idea who it wis. They're jeest passin this body across. He'd a white t-shirt on and a pair of jeans, whoever he wis, and they'd just tucked in his erms. One of his erms swung oot, this haun fawin doon and he had this tattoo…

1. … swallows. On his hand… and I goes, fuckin hell, that's Moosey. That's, ken, ma mate. Lying on the deck o the boat. Deid.

4. Of coorse we're aa staunin there gan, who is it? And I'm gan, god, I hope it's nae Davey cos even though the boat's gone doon and they've pit oot a mayday, even if ye canna find any trace, ye'r still hoping that they got in a life-raft or…

1. … speakin tae somebody one night then takin his body ashore the next.

2. Once you've picked up a body, that's when aabody thinks, Jesus Christ, ken?

3. We had tae lay him on fish boxes wi a tarpaulin ower the top an tie him in.

4. They widna tak him inside the boat.

2. They got Davey. And twa others. Four they found.

1. That wis my first experience of death at the fishing. Four found. Four lost. Aa deid.

4. I wis supposed tae be Davey's best man the followin week. And instead, I cerried him oot the kirk.

3. It wis a disaster for this toon.

A beat.

2. For weeks efter that, we were aa in a flippin daze. Ken? It's difficult tae comprehend that aa those young men, aa very fit men, couldna get off the boat.

7. And see efterwards – believe this if ye like – ye couldna hear nothin, nae even a bird singin in the toon.

5. Eight widows. Fourteen children.

6. Aa fowk wi mithers an faithers an freens an…

1. The water wis like glass the day efter it went doon. I'd never seen onythin like it.

The CHORUS group together. SKIPPER calls to SHONA.

SKIPPER	Div ye see fit ye'r dein? Trawlin up fit's been drooned in the salts o time.
SHONA	He was there that night. When the Grateful was lost.
VOICES	1. See? She wants her story. Nae oors.

20

6. Her story?

1. Aye, aboot the one taken fae her.

SKIPPER   Ah, but your story's hers and hers is yours.
            It's aa bound thegither.

SKIPPER produces a hipflask and passes it to SHONA.

            Here. Drink that tae loosen yer tongue.

SHONA hesitates.

            Ye can caw me Skipper.

She accepts the flask and takes a large sip.

            Better?

She nods. She turns to the CHORUS.

SHONA   My name's Shona.

The CHORUS whisper amongst themselves.

VOICES   5. Ach! I ken her. It's Jock's quine.

            1. Jock's quine, ye say?

            7. Oh aye. That's her.

            2. He wis a fine man.

A beat.

SHONA   Help me. Please. Talk to me.

            I need to know who he was. I need to know
            what happened.

SKIPPER   Aa knowledge comes wi a price.

SHONA   I'll do whatever it takes.

21

SKIPPER   Weel then, Miss Shona. We'll tell ye your
                 story.
                 We'll tell yours – if you listen tae oors.

The storm settles.

SCENE 3

SKIPPER gathers the CHORUS, a ringleader summoning the troupes.

SKIPPER   We'll need a family tae tell the tale.
                 A femily like ony other.
                 A mither, faither an twa brothers.

BILLY, KEVIN and JOCK step forward from the CHORUS.

BILLY tips his hat.

BILLY   Billy "Bilbo" MacInnes.

SKIPPER introduces BILLY to SHONA.

SKIPPER   That'd be yer grandfaither.

Then KEVIN.

KEVIN   Kevin "Tune" MacInnes.

SKIPPER   Yer uncle.

And, finally, JOCK.

JOCK   Jock "Jocko" MacInnes.

SKIPPER   And ye ken him.

A moment.

SHONA steps towards JOCK but he does not see her.

                 It disna work like that, quine. Ye canna get
                 in the wye o the story.

22

SHONA	I don't remember him.
SKIPPER	Ye will.

A beat.

> *(To the audience.)* So the Grateful went doon like mony afore.
> Each an ivery man and wife an bairn felt the rippling affect.

SKIPPER pours drams for the family.

SKIPPER	Tae the Grateful.
ALL	The Grateful.

They drink quietly; they are thoughtful, respectful.

BILLY	Eicht loons.
JOCK	We should be gan hame, dad.
BILLY	They shouldna have been oot in those watters. Nae in that boat, it wisna fit. That mannie wis leadin them tae their deaths.
JOCK	Mam'll be worried.
BILLY	We'll hae anither dram. Ane for ivery poor brute lost oot there.
SKIPPER	Ye'll need mare than the one bottle for that.

SKIPPER, handily, pulls out another.

> Wi good fortune, I came prepared.

JOCK	Dad. We need tae get hame.

KEVIN grabs his arm.

KEVIN	Jocko. Dinna be such a mammy's boy. She kens we're aaright.

KEVIN holds his glass out to SKIPPER and demands –

> Anither.

SKIPPER tops them up.

BILLY   Tae Davey.

SKIPPER   Davey!

KEVIN   Davey.

A beat.

JOCK   Tae Davey.

They quickly neck their drinks. SKIPPER tops them up again.

BILLY   Tae Moosey.

ALL   MOOSEY!

They hold out their glasses. A pause.

BILLY, KEVIN and JOCK stumble over to MEG (BILLY's wife). She is waiting for them. SKIPPER returns to the boat perch and gestures for SHONA to join.

BILLY   Ma wife! Ma bonnie, bonnie wife.

He attempts to kiss her.

SKIPPER   *(To the audience.)* Och, there'll be troubled winds thenight.

MEG   Whit time d'ye caw this? Ye were supposed tae be hame ooers ago.

BILLY   We were toastin – the loons.

MEG   When ye phoned, you said ye'd be back. Ye said nae tae panic, ye said that –

BILLY   Enough! I'm back. Yer loons are back. Mare
               than I can say for the poor buggers lost oot
               there.

MEG   And whit wid I be sayin if *you* were one o
               the poor buggers oot there? D'ye think I'd
               be happy seein boys oot pished an shoutin
               yer names? Dinna be such an insensitive
               eejit.

SKIPPER   Force 10 gales. Gye frosty.

*MEG turns to KEVIN and JOCK. She looks as though she may hug
them – but stops.*

MEG   I'm glad tae see ye'r baith safe. Kevin, ye'd
               better get back tae Kath.

KEVIN   One fer the road, Mam.

MEG   No. She'll be worried seek. She's nae as used
               tae this as I am.

KEVIN   Kath kens nothin bad'll happen tae me. I'm
               nae a fool.

MEG   Aye? Only a fool wid come oot wi somethin
               so bloody stupit! Where's yer heid at? Eight
               men died thenight. I'll hae nae mare o yer
               nonsense.

BILLY   He's had a few, leave him be.

MEG   And you? You should ken bloody better.

               (To KEVIN.) Go hame. Jeest go hame.

MEG turns to JOCK.

JOCK   Sorry, Mam.

A beat.

MEG   Dinna be saft. I'll see you themorn.

A moment.

                   Go. All of you. Get tae.

JOCK, KEVIN and BILLY rejoin the CHORUS.

SKIPPER   Sigh no more, lady, sigh no more,
                   Men were deceivers ever,
                   One foot in sea and one on shore.

SKIPPER touches MEG's shoulder; a musical moment.

A breath. A memory. She tells her story.

MEG   Eicht widows. Fourteen children. I ken whit
                   they'll be feelin thenicht.

                   My ain faither wis lost at the sea near twenty
                   year ago. I woke up that nicht gaspin fer
                   air. Gaspin. Billy wis awa at the sea an'aa.
                   I wis sittin in the hoose wi every light on
                   waitin fer them tae come and tell me that
                   somethin had happened. I kent somethin
                   had happened.

                   Ma pal Marie come doon tae tell me the
                   news. I was waitin for her, for them, for
                   someone tae arrive. The door wis open.
                   I'd unlocked the door. And I waited.

                   It wis 2 o'clock in the mornin, the time was
                   written doon, so the minute he...

A beat.

                   I sat waitin for them to come. And they did.

MEG rejoins the CHORUS.

VOICES   6. I saw it on the breakfast news.

2. Fuck. That's ma brother's boat.

1. A chap at the door.

7. The Mission man. Bearer o bad news.

4. I kent. I jeest kent.

SKIPPER *(To the audience.)* Christ. Ye can tell this'll be a cheery story, eh?
I'm needin a dram efter that.

SHONA I don't understand… if it was that bad… if it was that dangerous… why? Why did they do it?

SKIPPER Ye want the real story, ye spik tae the real men – follow the river an ye'll find the sea.

Come on – the pub. That'll get the lot o them gassin.

SCENE 4

The CHORUS make a basic pub using a few bar stools.

SHONA Tell me… how did it start?

The CHORUS share their stories.

VOICES 4. I jeest liked the idea o it. Ken, it wis like an adventure.

1. I think it's in oor blood. It must be.

2. Salt blood.

4. See, if yer faither went tae the sea then the femily jeest followed.

3. The boy used to come roon the secondary school an say:

27

2. *"What are you going to do when you leave the school?"*

3. Weel, I'm gan tae the fishin.

2. *"Oh, are you? Have you not thought about getting a trade?'*

3. Nah! I'm gan tae the fishin!

1. Aa these careers people comin in an, fit ye'r thinkin is: *you* think you're smart – but next year I'll be earnin the same money as you! I'll be earnin double the year efter. Treble the year efter that! Fa are you tae sit there an tell me fit I should dee?

4. We were ay doon the herbour muckin aboot.

3. Yer school jotter wis covered in drawins o boats.

2. I still draw pictures o the fishin boats.

3. You wid!

4. The bigger the waves the better I liked it. Jeest gan up an doon. This is unbelievable! Brilliant! Just sea. Couldna see nothin else cos the waves were massive.

1. Aa the loons were so intae it, ken? But yer mam wid say:

SKIPPER Ye'r nae gan tae the herbour!

VOICE 1. I'm nae gan tae the herbour.

 (To the audience.) She fuckin kens ye'r gan!

SKIPPER I'm nae stupid – ye come hame an ye'r smellin o fuckin fish!

28

VOICE	1. Fuckin stinkin. Honkin, like. As if she widna notice. Then when it came tae gettin a job, she says:
SKIPPER	Ye'r nae gan tae the fishin!
VOICE	1. We'd lost that mony people at the sea, ken? Then she says:
SKIPPER	I'll get ye a job onshore. No way ye'r gan tae the fishin!
VOICES	1. So, I ended up a joiner – but it wis difficult. These boys were comin hame wi nearly £200 a week an I wis gettin 30 quid. I could hardly buy a pint an they were buyin bottles o whisky! That's the reason I went.
	4. Aye. The fishin wis boomin.
	2. You got a berth on the best boat, made the money and that wis jeest the wye.
	3. The families that aabody looked up tae wis the skippers o the top boats... nae only were they dein well for themselves, they were gein employment tae other people.
	1. And *that* kept the villages alive.

Sound of the sea, a wave breaking.

SCENE 5

SKIPPER	The hands o time are salt rusted but we'll push them forward an inch. A femily gatherin. The ship o state an change o tide.
	All aboard!

The family members step out from the CHORUS. Firstly, MEG and BILLY. They are joined by JOCK and KEVIN. Finally, their respective wives, EVE and KATH. EVE is pregnant.

SKIPPER, accompanied by SHONA, weaves through the scene unnoticed.

SKIPPER   Cheers.

ALL   Cheers!

SKIPPER   Och, they like a good dram, this lot. I'm nae complainin.

KEVIN   Tae the aul man finally findin his legs on land.

JOCK   Leavin the waters, eh? Niver thocht I'd see this day.

BILLY   Noo, boys… it's nae really the end, I'll still go dee the prawns wi Tam sometimes.

MEG   You will *not*, Billy.

BILLY   How nae?

MEG   Nae chance. I've had enough o it. I'm nae washin onymare stinkin clase – even if ye pyed me. The doctor says ye have tae rest. Ye'r nae haulin nets onymare.

BILLY   They dinna haul nets noo, Meg! Aa this new-fangled technology. If they'd had that in the first place, I widna have done ma back in. I'd still hae a good twenty year o the watter in me.

MEG   Rubbish. Ye'll be lucky if you live that long, ye bugger.

KEVIN   Bilbo Billy… thief o the sea, stuck on land.

JOCK   Mam winna ken whit tae dee wi hersel noo
                ye'r back.

KEVIN   Ken, whit's the longest ye'v had him hame
                since you were merriet?

MEG   Since we were merriet? Christ, the minute
                we were oot the kirk he jumped back on the
                boat. Couldna get oota here fast enough.
                Anyone wid think I'd twisted his erm intae it
                the wye he ran. I wis worried o rumours
                I wis expectin.

BILLY   Fa's the faither, like?

MEG "claps his lug".

EVE   Well, I hope nae too much of it transfers to
                this one. I dinna want him born wi scales!

SHONA stands and the family freeze.

She walks towards EVE and reaches out to her stomach.

SHONA   *(To SKIPPER.)* Is that…?

SKIPPER   Aye.

The scene unfreezes. EVE touches her stomach.

A moment.

EVE   I'm hoping for a wee doctor or a lawyer in
                here.

KATH   That's a bit fancy noo, Eve. A doctor!

EVE   What's wrong with aiming high?

MEG   Nothin wrong wi a job on the ocean, ma
                quine. Look how these two turned out.

KEVIN   Aye. I'm gorgeous an he's a glaik.

JOCK	Wisen up!
KEVIN	Truth hurts, pal.
BILLY	Ach, you boys'll be grand – baith berths on the New Dawn, that's nothin tae turn yer nose up at.
EVE	I just worry if it'll be stable enough.
KEVIN	Fa needs stability?
EVE	We've the wee one to think about now.
KEVIN	Ye'll never win if ye dinna gamble.
MEG	When ye'r heid tae toe in diamonds an fur, ma quine, ye winna be sae worried.
KATH	I'd love a fur coat… pretty please, Kev?
KEVIN	Aye, aaright. If you wear nae knickers.
KATH	In front o yer mither…!
MEG	Ye fool brute.
BILLY	Wait til ye get your ain boat, loons.
KEVIN	Aye. That's when we'll be makin a mint – bloody fur coats aa aroon!
JOCK	It'll gee us freedom – tae dee whit we want, when we want.
KEVIN	Nae bosses, nae fuckers tellin us whit tae dee.
JOCK	Oor ain choice.
EVE	And you'll go back tae the West Coast.
JOCK	Aye.

EVE	Good. We'd maybe get to see you mare than once a fortnight.
KEVIN	Nae if the North Sea's still a treasure. We need tae be oot there fer the whites, the real whites, the big, fat money makers.
BILLY	There wisna cash like that in my days.
JOCK	Fa kens far the fishin will go. Aabody's sayin the money's in the oil[1] noo. Tam wis sayin if we got jobs –
KEVIN	Fuck Tam! The oil? Niver heard mare nonsense in ma life.
BILLY	Hear hear!
JOCK	Some of the boys are speakin aboot it, sayin they're gan tae go. Mare regular money.
KEVIN	Aye right. They'll dee twa month an come runnin back.
JOCK	I'm jeest sayin whit other fowk are sayin.
BILLY	Ken fit I'd say?

KEVIN and JOCK lean in.

Anither ane for the road!

He holds out his glass for a top up.

| MEG | Typical. I'm nae gan tae be yer bloody waitress noo, that's a given. |

She fills his glass. Seeing this, SKIPPER sticks their glass out for a top up.

| SKIPPER | Dinna mind if I do. |

---

[1]   Oil is most commonly prounounced as 'isle'.

SKIPPER stands at the side of the group but remains unnoticed.

KEVIN   Pile o pish, aa this oil chat.

JOCK   *(To EVE.)* Did ye ever hear dad's story aboot
                Jamesy Giant and the lightning?

EVE   No, don't think so. Sounds like a bairn's
                book.

KATH   Oh, it's a good ane.

KEVIN   I'll show them where the money's at.

MEG   *(To EVE.)* His stories... watch they dinna hae
                erms and legs attached.

                (Whispers.) And a willy an'aa.

BILLY   Haud yer wheesht, woman!

KEVIN   *(To JOCK.)* And it's nae in the bloody West
                Coast either.

BILLY   Pipe doon, wid ye? Right. Jamesy Giant –

KEVIN   Oh fer fucks sake –

Everyone glowers at him – a reaction.

                Fine. Fine!

BILLY   Jamesy Giant and the lightnin.

The performance begins.

                We used tae land the fish on the aul railway
                pier. It wis aa railway sleepers, ken? And
                we were landin fish on a Sunday night an
                Jamesy Giant... d'ye ken him, Eve?

EVE   Not sure?

MEG   Aye ye dee. Ken Marky McKay?

34

EVE   No?

BILLY   Aye ye ken Marky McKay! He's the ane wi
               the twinnies. Mark's their faither? Ye ken him.

EVE   I know the twins that bide near the pub.

MEG   No, no, no. Nae them. The other twins. The
               bald anes! They're aboot fifty noo.

KEVIN   *(Reluctantly.)* Ye'll hae seen them in the pub.

JOCK   They were there the night o Kenny's
               birthday.

KATH   Aye, they were there, that's right.

EVE   I'll maybe have seen them in the pub.

MEG   Right. Weel, ken Bessie? Bessie Bobby
               Byers? That's her man.

EVE   One of the twins?

MEG   No! Mark's her man. He wis skipper o the
               Damsel. Marky McKay. The auler twin's
               married tae a McKenzie... at the bottom of
               the brae across fae Jimmy.

EVE   Don't know if I know...

MEG   Well, Maria, that's his wife's name. Maria
               McKenzie. Droll wifey. Ye'll have seen her
               in the Post Office, ay wearin a floorey hat.

BILLY   Right. Ken when you go doon the brae, the
               hooses at the bottom? Same street as the
               Gregor's bide on but further across.

EVE looks at JOCK for help.

JOCK   Near Jeanie's.

KATH	They've got that funny yella gate.
EVE	Ah! Gotcha.
SKIPPER	Christ.
EVE	Okay. So this Marky McKay…?
BILLY	No, nae him. Ane o his loons. Mini Twinnie.
EVE	Married tae… Maria?
MEG	No, the other ane. Mini Twinnie. He never merriet.
EVE	Right.
BILLY	Fit wis I saying? Ye'v raveled me.
SKIPPER	Ye'r nae the only ane.
JOCK	The story aboot Jamesy Giant an the lightnin.
BILLY	Right. So, Mini Twinnie –
EVE	Mini Twinnie. The – son?
BILLY	Aye. Mini Twinnie wis skipperin this boat that Giant wis on, right? An he wis staunin on the pier –
JOCK	He means Giant. Giant wis standin on the pier.
BILLY	Aye, okay! *Giant* wis staunin on the pier. And we're aa wi oor oilskins soakin weet an this, right, jeest this almighty flash o lightnin, ken? And it burnt fae aboot there…

A short distance.

> … tae there awa fae him. Jeest a huge burn wi this flash o lightnin. And he jeest went –

36

Flash of lightning near SKIPPER.

SKIPPER	Missed ye bastard!
MEG	Missed ye bastard!

MEG has stolen BILLY's punchline.

BILLY	Missed ye bastard…

A pause.

MEG	Pity it missed the bastard.
SKIPPER	Ah ha!
JOCK	Mam!
MEG	Weel! He'd fecht wi his ain shadow that mannie. And his brother Willy wis a drunken eejit. And Shirley, well, she wis jeest bloody wicked.
JOCK	Dinna haud back, mam.
MEG	She looked like a fuckin cod! A foushty cod, at that. Poor craiter. I'll nae hide it, Jock, that wis a femily o glaiks. Anywye… that loon's deid noo.
EVE	Giant?
MEG	No! Marky.
EVE	Oh… right.

EVE looks at JOCK for help again.

JOCK	Ye'll figure oot who aabody is in nae time – far their hoose is, fa their mither wis –
KEVIN	Fa's shaggin fa.
MEG	Fer the love o God.

KEVIN	*(To KATH.)* It's like ane o your bloody soap operas roon here.
BILLY	Ach. I'm gan tae miss it aaright. The stories. The life. The end o an era.
KEVIN	And the start o a new ane.
JOCK	A new bairn, a new boat.
BILLY	Ye'r a lucky man. Fit I widna gee tae be startin ower again. Ach weel, at least I've got you loons tae cerry on the good name.
KEVIN	That ye dee. First the New Dawn –
BILLY	Then yer ain boat.
JOCK	That's the goal.
KEVIN	*(To JOCK.)* Naethin's gan tae stop us, brother. You an me –
BILLY	Nae that again.
KEVIN	Aye, how nae? Femily motto.
BILLY	It wis fine when you were five but nae noo.
KEVIN	Gaan, Jocko. You and me –

This has obviously been rehearsed.

KEVIN / JOCK   – versus the sea.

They shake hands.

SCENE 6

SKIPPER   A pause for a wee poem aboot the bynames.

Right. You've Bilbo Billy and Kevin the
Tune...
Jock's jeest Jocko, the youngest loon.
But it's nae jeest your family in this wee toon.
There's Jerky and Sweaty an Hamish Blah,
Blackie and Bitters an Buntin an'aa.
There's Shagger and Dagger, Sheepy an Juice,
Guerny and Porno, Rascal an Woose.
Dichty and Lichty, Mighty an Shitey,
Bob the gob, Big Lils and Blighty.
Nellie, Welly, Smelly an Giant James...
For every cheil, there'll be twa names.

He bows to the audience and SHONA.

SCENE 7

Sound of the sea, wind howling; a storm.

The CHORUS share their stories with SHONA.

VOICES 1. We couldna hae been fishin for mare than
ten ooers when this gale comes awa.

3. I'm on watch gan: whit the hell is that?
It's comin closer an closer an closer then
bang! It hits us. A fuckin hurricane!

1. The boat's gan aa ower the place, watter
everywhere – radar winna turn, the wind
wis that strong, nae idea far we were fer
aboot eight, nine ooers... in darkness.

4. Dancin aboot like a wee cot, watter
everywhere.

Sound of the storm building.

2. We gets through the night an took a couple of real serious lumps o watter on the deck. Get tae Oban an there's boats sunk everywhere.

1. And there's the light-hoose ship moved intae the middle of the bay and dropped her anchor and aa the boats tied tae it – like chickens tae a mother hen.

2. My hair went grey that night. That's true.

3. One blast o wind… the tail end of a hurricane an boats scattered everywhere. Everythin damaged.

2. Ye jeest go, wow… that's power.

1. That's how a fisherman came hame, showered, changed clase an went straight tae the bar. Get pished the first day back.

4. The pub wis fill o fishermen. Aa jeest lettin off steam.

1. Gettin steamin, aye!

2. Fit a relief tae get back hame.

The CHORUS settle leaving JOCK and EVE, KEVIN and KATH in the pub together.

SHONA sits with SKIPPER.

JOCK	Ye'r leavin the New Dawn.
KEVIN	Bigger an better things, Jocko.
JOCK	Aye – for you maybe.
KEVIN	Aa in the good name o the femily.

JOCK	I thocht femily stuck thegither? We're meant tae be a team. You and me – (versus the sea)
KEVIN	A couple years apairt will dee us good.
JOCK	Ye mean it'll do *you* good.
KEVIN	I've been offered a damned good opportunity, I'm nae turnin it doon.
EVE	What aboot gettin your own boat?
KEVIN	Look. I'm bein offered mate on the Trident. Jocko will probably get mate on the New Dawn wi me gone. We'll baith get mare money. It maks sense.
JOCK	It's nae aa aboot the money.
KATH	*(To EVE.)* They took ower a grand their last trip. It would be stupid for him nae tae tak it.
JOCK	An aboot three months ago, they were in the shit. Ye canna judge it on the last trip. We need tae be lookin tae the future.
KEVIN	I *am* lookin tae the future – I'm lookin tae the future of *ma femily*.
JOCK	Far does that leave me?
KEVIN	We're nae bairns anymare, I shouldna need tae haud yer haun.
JOCK	Aa this, workin on the New Dawn, wis for one reason and one reason only – for savin up and gettin oor ain boat.
KEVIN	Dinna be jealous cos I got offered it and you didna.

41

JOCK	We had a plan! Kev – I canna spend my hale life dodgin aroon whitever decisions tak yer fancy.
KEVIN	My ain fuckin brother, the blue-eyed boy – I kent you'd be jealous. I kent it.
EVE	Kevin – you don't have to / (get so angry)
KEVIN	/ Nae need for *you* tae stick yer nose in.
JOCK	Dinna speak to her like that.
KEVIN	She disna ken her erse fae her elbow when it comes tae the sea.

(To EVE.) Ye should mind yer ain fuckin business. |
EVE	This is my business!
KATH	*(To KEVIN.)* Calm doon. It's nae worth this.
KEVIN	And dinna you start tellin me whit tae dee either.
JOCK	Kevin. If it's whit ye want, on ye go – I canna stop you. I jeest thought if one of us wis leavin, we both wid. We'll dee it in a couple of years like ye said. Right? Nae need tae be a dick aboot it.
KEVIN	We're gan hame tae celebrate. Kath, neck that an get yer coat.

KATH looks at EVE and JOCK. She finishes her drink and puts on her coat. There's an awkward pause.

Kath.

KATH	I'll phone ye themorn, Eve.

EVE	Aye, okay.
KATH	Goodnight.
EVE	Night.
JOCK	Night.

KEVIN tries to exit but SKIPPER blocks his path.

SKIPPER	Anither round?

SKIPPER rings a boxing style bell.

KEVIN looks back at JOCK. He grabs KATH's hand and exits.

(To the audience.) One path becomes two, one femily broken in half. Promises made and severed.

A moment.

JOCK	I'm sorry.
EVE	It's nae your fault.

A beat.

He'll niver see past me bein an incomer.

JOCK	Ye'r ma wife. Ye'r part o this femily.
EVE	I'm trying.
JOCK	Ye dinna need tae *try*. Ye'r stuck wi me. For better – and worse.

A beat.

I dinna ken whit I'd dee withoot ye.

EVE	Probably starve.

A beat.

	Kevin will come roon. Let him have his few trips on the Trident and he'll see sense.
JOCK	Looks like it'll be a whiley afore I get tae spend time wi the bairn.
EVE	She'll be fine. You'll get the boat by the time she's in school so you'll be back at weekends. You can help with her homework... you'll be desperate to get away again.
JOCK	I'm gan tae miss her growin up. Whit's the point in haein a femily if ye niver see them?
EVE	There's nothin we can do about it. You canna afford to get the boat on your own, you'll just have tae bide your time.

EVE takes JOCK's hand.

| JOCK | My hale life has been tied up wi Kevin's. Disna metter whit I dee... I canna seem tae brak awa. |
| EVE | Blood's thicker than water. He'll ay be a part of yer world. |

A moment.

JOCK	Eve. I want ye tae promise me somethin.
EVE	What?
JOCK	I want ye tae promise me.
EVE	Aye, okay, I will – but tell me what it is first.
JOCK	Trust me. Go on. Say ye'll promise.
EVE	Right, fine. I promise. Now whit am I actually promising tae do?

A beat.

JOCK	If onythin ever happens tae me… you'll move on.
EVE	What?
JOCK	If onythin ever happens tae me.
EVE	Where's this coming from?
JOCK	I'm askin ye tae promise.
EVE	Don't even dare say it again.

She shoves JOCK playfully.

Nothin's gan to happen to you, ye eejit. Whit would make you say that?

JOCK	Everythin jeest feels – oot o ma control.
EVE	It'll get better. *That* I can promise you.

Come on. Enough o the doom an gloom. Take me home.

JOCK	Is that an order, Mrs?
EVE	Aye. And dinna make me ask twice.
JOCK	Weel, when you pit it like that…

JOCK picks EVE up and spins her around.

Hame it is.

They begin to exit watched by SKIPPER and SHONA.

SHONA	Wait!

She walks to EVE, her mother.

He made you promise?

45

EVE   Aye. He did.

EVE reaches out and squeezes her daughter's hand.

EVE and JOCK exit.

SHONA   *(To SKIPPER.)* Did he know?

SKIPPER   Ye'r wonderin if he had a premonition?
                Dreamt o the sea swallowin him in the black
                o the nicht?

                We ay listened tae dreams in ma day.
                Omens. That's fit we caad them.
                Watched oot an listened fer signs it was yer
                time.

SHONA   Was it my dad's time?

SKIPPER doesn't answer.

                Was it his time?

SKIPPER still doesn't answer.

                            SCENE 8

Sequence of men working at the sea, acted out by the CHORUS.

A working tune. Perhaps a song.

SKIPPER   A fishing boat is a weird environment. You
                go back on a Sunday night, open the galley
                door and –

SKIPPER opens the galley door for SHONA.

SHONA   Eugh!

SKIPPER   Fish brains and diesel.

SHONA   That's disgusting.

VOICES	1. Efter a few days you didna notice it.
	2. When ye'r there, ye dinna smell yoursel cos aabody else smells the same.
	3. To be clean, ye just need to be cleaner than the guy sittin next tae ye.
	1. But, if ye came in contact with anyone that had showered, they'd think: awww, ye'r absolutely honkin!
	4. There wis a kind o excitement at times aboot it. Excitement at seein a bag o fish comin up.
	2. Ye didna ken if you were gan tae get a lot of fish or a wee droppy fish…
	3. Especially cod!
SKIPPER	The "green". The money fish.
VOICES	1. The net hits the surface an ye go, wow! Look at that.

The nets are hauled, revealing that they are full of money.

4. Excitement… definitely an excitement!

They divide up the cash.

2. Coorse, there's ay the dangerous side –

1. – a lump o water tryin to tak you awa wi it.

ALL   Holy fuck!

They duck.

VOICES   3. But when ye'r young –

They shrug and continue to work.

1. Then there wis the scalders.

SHONA   Scalders?

VOICES   2. Jellyfish!

1. We'd hae tae wear hats so we widna get
scalders comin ontae oor faces.

Someone is stung – a reaction.

2. The strands from these jellyfish wid
go intae yer een… you couldna protect
yourself. Yer face wid be burnin.

4. There wis only seven of you on the boat
so ye could never faw oot wi onybody. How
could ye stay clear o somebody you fell oot
wi? If onybody did really faw oot, one wid
leave cos, well, whit's the point?

A fight breaks out.

3. It's bad enough bein at the sea but fawin
oot maks yer life unbearable.

1. An atmosphere on a 70ft boat.

SKIPPER   Far are ye meant tae go?

VOICES   1. Stuck oot there for a week.

2. I've seen us awa fifteen days! Seein nothin
but ocean. Nae much of a life compared tae
workin in the West Coast. Nae for a young
lad onywye.

3. Three, four days withoot gan tae oor bed.

1. One time we shot an got a big first haul
an we worked on oor feet for near 70 hours
afore we got to our beds.

2. Ye'r guttin, ye'r washin fish… it's an oot o body experience. If anyone had seen us in that last few hours they'd have thocht we were aa pished.

1. Work, work, work.

4. Slower and slower.

1. Work, work, work.

3. Cat nap. Sleep a wee bit in yer oilies.

1. Work, work, work.

2. I mind bein in the wheelhoose an speakin tae this other skipper, right? Wonderin why I wisna gettin a reply. I wis talkin intae ma coffee cup.

4. Ye get used tae haein an ooer or two of sleep. It's different.

1. Fishermen are different.

2. You get this look, this gaunt look. Yer body wis done.

1. Whit we used tae dee, you widna believe. You widna believe the work. But you didna ken ony better.

The boat rests at the harbour. JOCK gets off of it and makes his way to the wee sheddie. He is exhausted. SHONA watches.

SKIPPER   A dram?

JOCK   Aye. Alright.

SKIPPER produces a bottle and pours a dram for them both.

SKIPPER   Tough trip?

JOCK   Twelve days. I'm needin hame tae see ma
                bairn.

He necks the dram.

SKIPPER   Ye'll nae stay for one mare?

JOCK   Aye, okay. One mare then hame.

KEVIN enters and joins SKIPPER and JOCK.

SKIPPER   Oh, I ken ye'll tak a dram.

He pours three nips.

KEVIN   Of coorse.

JOCK   Good trip?

KEVIN   Ower a grand in ma back pocket, brother.
                I hear ye'r nae far off.

JOCK nods.

                We should be celebratin! Prime Minister's
                makin 40k an I'm nae far behind. And she
                has a fuckin country to run.

JOCK   Quotas nae affectin ye?

KEVIN   Quotas can fuck right off.

JOCK finishes his dram and stands.

JOCK   I'm gan hame.

KEVIN   Ach, come on. The pub for a few. That
                young lassie wi the nice tits'll maybe be
                workin.

A beat.

	C'mon. Lighten up, min. We'll start plannin buying the boat. Gee it anither year an we'll be there.
JOCK	Anither year, I ken. Ye'v said it afore.
	I've got tae get hame.
KEVIN	Phone Eve later, tell her ye'v just landed. A pint an a perv, whit mare could ye want?
JOCK	Enjoy yersel.
KEVIN	Ye need to start buyin her mare jewellery. Kath doesna care when I get back if I pick up somethin shiny.
JOCK	Denner at Mam's themorn?
KEVIN	Aye. She'll gee me a lugfill if I miss it.

JOCK exits.

	(To SKIPPER.) You'll be comin tae the pub, aye?
SKIPPER	Ye widna hae to ask me twice.

SKIPPER nods to SHONA.

| | This ane's comin an'aa. |

A beat.

KEVIN	*(To SHONA.)* You look familiar.
SHONA	Do I?
SKIPPER	Ane o them faces, eh kiddo? Ane of them faces that'll haunt ye til ye figure it oot.

KEVIN stares at SHONA.

A moment.

KEVIN   I'll get a round in.

KEVIN exits.

SHONA   Why don't I trust him?

SKIPPER   One word: money.
                 The smell o diesel, the reek o fish…
                 the stink o money.

SCENE 9

BILLY and MEG's house.

A family gathering – JOCK and EVE, KEVIN and KATH. SKIPPER and SHONA watch.

BILLY   I'll say somethin for ye, Meggie. You mak a
                 grand denner.

MEG   Is that aa I'm good for noo?

JOCK   Winna be able to move for a week.

KEVIN   Fat bastard.

MEG   Och, I ken you'll baith be back for seconds in
                 a minutey. Right, fa's for a cup o tea? Billy?

BILLY   I'm haein a dram. Loons?

On hearing "dram" SKIPPER grabs a glass and joins the men.

MEG   Right, sort yerselves. Quines? Cup o tea?

EVE   Oh aye, that'd be magic, thanks Meg.

KATH   Aye, ta.

                 You alright, Eve? Ye'r lookin a wee bitty
                 peely-wally.

EVE	Fine, aye. I've had a wee bit of the flu ongoing, you know?
MEG	Ye eatin right?
EVE	Aye, course I am.
MEG	Nothin on ye. You look like a frozen shit –
JOCK	Mam!
MEG	Weel! She's skin an bones.
JOCK	I think ye look beautiful.
EVE	Thank you.

The men stand to one side pouring drams, MEG, EVE and KATH gather together. There is a clear gender divide.

MEG	Right. How ye wantin yer tea?
EVE	Just black.
MEG	Nae milk?
KATH	I'll hae milk.
MEG	Nae milk for you, Eve?
EVE	Nah, just black, thank you.
MEG	A piece?
EVE	No, no.
MEG	How no?
EVE	I'm stuffed.
MEG	I kent it! Ye'r dietin again, aren't you? That's how ye'r lookin sae pale.

53

KATH	Are ye dietin, Eve? Ye didna tell me ye were dietin. Whit ain are ye dein?
EVE	I'm not, I'm just nae hungry.
MEG	Ye nae wantin a snowball?
EVE	Honestly, I'm fine.
MEG	A Penguin?
KATH	Ooh, I'll tak a Penguin.
EVE	No. Thank you.
MEG	Loons? A Penguin?
JOCK	No ta, Ma.
BILLY	Nae wi a dram, wifie. Will ye stop yer nippin?
MEG	Watch yer moo or ye'll be in for a slap, bugger lugs.
	(To EVE.) Right. Fruit loaf? Malt loaf?
EVE	I'm fine.
MEG	Rich tea? Digestive?
EVE	Meg, I don't want a – (biscuit)
MEG	Shortbread! I've got some shortbread!
KATH	No, actually, I'll hae shortbread instead o a Penguin.
MEG	Right, shortbread. I'll get you quines some shortbread.
EVE	I really dinna want anything.

A beat.

MEG	Weel. I'll pit oot a plate onywye. Jeest in case.

MEG busies herself arranging a plate of biscuits.

Nothin wrong wi haein a biscuit wi yer tea.

She holds the tray out.

Ane's nae gan tae kill ye.

EVE	Fine. Fine. I'll have a snowball.

SKIPPER also appears next to the tray of biscuits and takes some before returning to the boat perch. The stash is shared with SHONA.

BILLY	Aa settled intae the new place, Jocko?
JOCK	Aye, gettin there.
BILLY	Look at you, ma loons. Baith wi yer ain hames, nae a cooncil hoose in sicht. I'm proud of ye.
KEVIN	That dram's gan tae your heid, aul man!
JOCK	I'm jeest nae gettin tae see it much.
KEVIN	Dinna start.
BILLY	Fit's for ye winna go by ye.
	(To KEVIN.) Ye'r still wantin tae wait?
KEVIN	Another year, that's aa. A year o dein some skipperin an I'll ken aa there is afore we invest. Is that nae – sensible?
JOCK	Except ye said that last year. And the one afore.
KEVIN	The Trident's where the money's at aynoo, okay?
BILLY	Money winna buy yer freedom, loon.

KEVIN   I ken that, eh? Soon. Right, Jocko?

JOCK   Ye ken I'm ready when you are.

The family continue drinking but our attention turns to SHONA and SKIPPER.

SHONA   Why did he want to wait?

SKIPPER   He wis on a top boat – aabody wanted tae
               go on one o them.
               Crazy days. Workin further awa.
               Mare money, mare danger.
               Work hard, live hard.

               An, ye see, apairt fae the money, there wis a
               certain –

               (To KEVIN.) – fit wid ye say?

KEVIN   Social status.

SKIPPER   Social. Status.

SHONA walks over to JOCK. The family don't notice her.

SHONA   Was my dad on one of these top boats?

SKIPPER   Kevin offered him a berth on the Trident
               that very nicht.

KEVIN   Weel?

JOCK   I dinna ken whit tae say.

KEVIN   Ye wanted tae fish thegither, didn't ye?

JOCK   Aye – but on oor ain boat.

KEVIN   We'll get there. A couple o trips on the
               Trident and ye'll be rollin in it. Ye'll see whit
               I mean. C'mon, Jocko.

You an me …

KEVIN holds out his hand.

A beat.

JOCK   … versus the sea.

They shake hands.

SKIPPER   Fate wis sealed.

A moment.

SHONA   It could have been a different story.

SKIPPER   No. This story will ay be the same.

SCENE 10

Heavy fog. The female CHORUS gather.

VOICES (FEMALE)

> 5. I can ay mind the weather when it wis bad,
> ken? If yer femily wis at the sea, ye ay worried.
>
> 6. They go oot in weather like that an they
> must wonder whether they'll come back or no.
>
> 5. But they couldna think like that. They
> widna hae went if they did.
>
> 7. I never heard my granda speakin aboot
> the weather, the bad weather. Because he
> widna want you tae worry aboot it.
>
> He'd maybe say:

SKIPPER   Aye, it was gye rough, roch this week.

VOICES (FEMALE)

7. Take oota that whit ye want!

5. "Roch kind this week".

6. You'd niver hear aboot it. But ye'd look oot the back windae and, ye'd just go –

5. – oh my goodness… they're oot there in the middle o that ocean in a little wee boatie. Ken?

7. Oh, Christ aye. You wid imagine the boat in aa that weathers.

6. Ye'r lying in yer bed hearin the wind and ye'r thinkin… God, I hope they're okay, I hope they're in somewhere or dodgin.

7. Livin on knife-edge aa the time.

6. Ay worried if there wis a gale o wind. But ye lived wi it. Ye had tae.

5. Ye jeest prayed that they were safe.

EVE and KATH step out from the CHORUS. SHONA and SKIPPER watch.

KATH	Ye'r really lookin for a joabbie?
EVE	Aye. Shona's gan to school soon. It'll be good for me.
KATH	But surely Jock's makin enough money? The Trident's earnin a fortune.
EVE	It's nae about the money. It's mare for me. I miss it. I really do.
KATH	You widna see me dein that. Nae chance.

EVE	Maybe next year I'll start a bit of studying an'aa. I'd love to get a qualification.
KATH	Honestly Eve, whit ye needin a *qualification* for?
EVE	Shona'll grow up one day... and I want tae be dein somethin when she does. I don't know – maybe business or hotel management.
KATH	Management? I canna understaun why ye'd want tae.
EVE	I don't like the sittin around... and they're away that much these days. Maybe once they're back West it'll be different. Anyway, I can study when the bairn's gone tae bed.
KATH	Well, it's your life, I guess. Nae whit I'd want.

A beat.

EVE	I didna know what bein a fisherman's wife would really be like. You know? Not really. I wisna brought up with it. I didn't know that you'd have to wait around for them to come home. And that they're nae sooner back an they're away again. And it's gettin worse – every trip is longer than the one afore.
	I guess I never really thought aboot it. I was young and stupid and...
KATH	Dinna say "in love".
EVE	Aye, well... I was.
KATH	Was?

A pause.

59

	Have you two had a fight?
EVE	No, no… it's just… it's nae easy, Kath. You know that.
KATH	The sea's their life. That's whit you've got tae accept.
EVE	Maybe Kev feels that way but Jock doesna.
KATH	Is this aboot that bloody boat again?

A beat.

EVE	Do you know Jock took a trip off a couple of weeks ago?
KATH	Tae dee his ticket exams? Aye.

A beat.

EVE	He went for an oil job.
KATH	Whit?
EVE	A job at the oil. He hates it, Kath. He loves the sea but he hates the life. He doesn't want to be stuck anymore. So… he decided to do somethin about it.
KATH	The oil? So he wis gan tae leave Kev in the lurch?
EVE	He canna wait around for him forever.
KATH	They're supposed to be workin thegither, I thought that's whit Jock wanted! When wis he gan tae tell him?
EVE	He's not. He went tae the interview. But he didna get it.
	At least he tried.

KATH	So, whit? He doesna want tae get a boat anymore? He's banged on aboot it for long enough.
EVE	Of course he wants it, it's all he knows! But he doesna want tae sit around an wait forever.
KATH	He doesn't? Or you dinna want him tae?

A beat.

	Ye canna just come somewhere like this and think ye can change aabody. You're the same as the rest o us noo, Eve, whether ye think it or no.
EVE	Dinna be like that. I'm talkin to you as a friend.
	Whatever's happened between them afore, we've ay been okay, haven't we? I'm tellin you that he doesn't want to do that job anymore. The work is madness. Kev must feel it too.

A beat.

KATH	I'm sorry it didna work oot for him.
EVE	Aye. Me too.

A musical moment.

SKIPPER reaches out and touches KATH's shoulder.

A breath. A story.

KATH	Eve wisna aroon when the fishin wis bad. She disna get it. This life. She disna ken whit it's like tae wait for yer man tae come hame

and then seein nothin but a desperate face…
an empty, exhausted face and nae cash.

Ma son Keith was born in the December
an William wis barely oota nappies. Noo,
it must've been March afore I got another
decent wage. That's a long, long time to dee
athoot money. But if the boat wisna makin
onythin, it wisna makin onythin.

Kev wis aaright when he wis awa, he wis
gettin fed on the boat. I lived on Rice
Krispies. I made sure the bairns got milk,
I ay made sure they had milk. We scrimped
by. As you dee. We jeest had tae survive.

That's the life she disna ken. And I widna
wish it on her.

SCENE 11

EVE and JOCK. SHONA and SKIPPER observe.

EVE	How did it go?
JOCK	He's ready. We're lookin for a boat, trip efter next.

EVE hugs JOCK.

EVE	I canna believe it. Finally. Finally! A new start. For you. For us. We should celebrate.

A beat.

	Whit's that face for?
JOCK	I'm fine.
EVE	Jock. Talk to me.

A beat.

JOCK	Div ye ken why they caw Kevin 'Tune'…?
EVE	Because – he likes music?
JOCK	Aabody likes music.
	It's cos if anyone had a problem oot there or he thocht they were moanin… he'd shout tae turn the tunes up. He never wanted tae listen tae onybody. Dad geed him the name years ago. Daft, I ken, but…
	Onyroad. Ane o the loons got a dunt on the heid this trip and Kev didna even get the first aid box oot. I'm there, tryin tae find oot whit happened and, ken whit he says? Turn up the tunes up an get on wi it.
	Poor boy's heid is pissin wi blood an Kev's got Eye of the Tiger blaring oot on the radio.
EVE	He's never exactly been kent for his bedside manner.

A beat.

JOCK	It wis ayways gan tae be the two o us pair skipperin, ken? Wi this boat. We've spoken aboot it since we were wee. Oor hale lives. But see workin wi him lately? He's changed. He's nae the same loon.
EVE	His temper's got worse.
JOCK	Aye. And he's already startin tae go on aboot percents… wantin tae pay the loons less an aa that bollocks.

EVE	There'll be nae need for him tae cheat anybody if you're makin enough money.
JOCK	But it's nae the wye I want tae dee things. Jeest – total greed. He's gan to be skimmin money off for this and that an the next thing.
EVE	You won't let him. You're nae like that.
JOCK	I dinna want tae be one o the buggers.
EVE	You winna be, ye haven't got it in you.
JOCK	I want tae be decent.
EVE	Then ye need to stand up tae him.

A beat.

JOCK	I wish I'd got intae the oil. I really fuckin do.
EVE	You ken what your dad ay says – "whit's for you won't go by you".
	It'll work out.
JOCK	I'll be fair. I'll ay try.
EVE	Me and Shona, we're proud of you – whatever ye decide.

A moment.

SKIPPER	Twa brothers.
	One born by the licht of day an one born tae the nicht. Baith wi salt blood runnin through their veins.
	Fit next for these two we've watched sail the tide? Wid they have been good and fair…? We'll never really know, will we? We'll never really know.

(Sung.) Oh, the lady is hungry...
She's callin tae me.
A drap o blood's needed...
Fa will it be...?

SCENE 12

SHONA and SKIPPER watch BILLY and MEG. There is a distance between them; they are in the past, the present and the in-between.

SKIPPER   Ye want tae see?

SHONA   Yes.

MEG   They were buyin the boat. It wis whit they'd
              ayways spoken aboot since they were wee
              bairns. He came to Billy, y'ken. He came tae
              him an said he wis worried aboot Kevin.
              He said:

JOCK enters.

JOCK   I dinna want tae pit ye in a bad position,
              dad. I'm sorry.

BILLY   No, no, ma loon. Fit is it ye'r needin?

              (To SHONA.) And he telt me. He telt me he
              wis worried. He telt me that he wisna sure
              how it wis gan tae work wi the twa of them
              skipperin the boat. He wis that nervous
              aboot it.

MEG   He ay wanted tae dee the right thing, oor
              Jock.

JOCK   I dinna want tae be a crook.

BILLY	You'll niver be a crook, ma loon. Ye'r too damned saft. Dinna gee up on Kev, he's jeest lost his wye a wee bit.
	(To SHONA.) An then he wis leavin. Off on the Trident again. They only had a few mare trips left, him and Kev, the wye things were gan wi the new boat.
	As he wis leavin, he turned an he said:
JOCK	I jeest want tae be fair. Like you were.
BILLY	*(To SHONA.)* And I went tae hug him. Hadna done that in years, ken? Dinna ken fit came ower me.
	And, instead, I said tae him…

MEG crosses into the past. She puts her hand on his arm.

I'm aaright.

Instead… I turned roon an I said tae him:

(To JOCK.) Fit's for you winna go by you, ma loon. Niver forget that.

(To SHONA.) That's whit I telt him. Fit's for you won't go by you.

The family rejoin the CHORUS. The stage is engulfed by the sight and sound of the sea. SHONA is somehow blocked from witnessing the following.

JOCK, KEVIN, SKIPPER and MATE are on the boat. The water begins to curl, crashing and roaring. It's difficult to see precisely what's happening – fragments of action, moments in time.

The wind howls, whipping up into a storm. Man versus the elements.

The fishermen gather – there seems to be a problem with the nets – and start hauling manually. They pull them and then they go back over – tug of war. A violent struggle as the nets are dragged back into the water. A glimpse of chaos. The fishermen fighting the ocean.

Suddenly, JOCK is gone.

The crash of a wave and darkness; a collage of search lights, the sound of the sea intertwined with screaming voices, a mayday call and a search helicopter. Panic.

A sudden dull silence.

The following speech could be delivered live or as a voiceover.

JOCK   You get on top of a wave an it sucks ye back doon.

              Voices. Peddlin. Shoutin. Crashin. Waves. Survival.
              The watter washes ye further away.
              Tired.
              Really tired.
              The bairn.
              Eve.
              Fight.
              Survive.

              Lie back and go tae sleep.

Pause.

              They say droonin is horrible.
              It's nae.

              Lie back and sleep.

              Sleep.

Darkness.

ACT 2

SCENE 13

The sound of the sea. A heavy fog.

SHONA stands alone. SKIPPER watches her.

SHONA   I look back and I see darkness.
There's a thick fog blocking the path into
my past.
An emptiness.

I wanted to reach into the depths and to find
the missing piece.
I wanted to free myself from the anchor
pulling me into the shadows.
I wanted to move forward.

I tried to build a life; a career, a home.
I tried to love.
I tried to plaster over, to hide, to run.
To hope.

But no matter what I did, no matter where I
went…
there was a sense, a feeling.
I couldn't escape –

ALL   The voices.

The CHORUS whisper.

SHONA   I was a journalist. I had a piece of paper
claiming I knew how to research and find facts.

I took a sabbatical from work, handed in my
notice for my flat and came home.

I didn't know if anyone would talk. But I had to try.

I had to try to remember.

SKIPPER places a hand on SHONA's shoulder.

A breath. A memory.

Fresh salty air. Brisk whipping wind. The plants in our garden wouldn't grow because of the sand in the soil. Watching dolphins jump, walking the dog through the rocky back-shore and the sandy front-shore. Building sand-castles. Sunbathing, paddling, swimming drunk as a teenager.

SKIPPER   The great unknown. A provider and taker of life. Oor lady o glory and tragedy.

SHONA   Lost at sea.

I've said it so many times before and I still don't know what it means. It sounds – poetic.

SKIPPER   Full fathom five thy father lies;
               Try, try.

SHONA   Unsure. Lost. No ending.
               Who, what, where, why, when?

SKIPPER   Of his bones are coral made;

SHONA   I knew nothing.
               There was an accident. A memorial.
               I missed him.
               Or I missed the idea of him because I
               couldn't remember.

SKIPPER   Those are pearls that were his eyes;

SHONA	A memory. Of playing hide and seek. I was hiding.
	I wish I'd known to treasure those short moments. I wish I'd been old enough to keep a diary or take pictures.
SKIPPER	Nothing of him that does fade,
SHONA	I pretended there was an underwater world and my dad was a part of it. It's easy to dream. Missing in action. Lost at sea. Where are they? Where does the body end up?
SKIPPER	But doth suffer a sea-change,
SHONA	What does it feel like to be in the middle of nowhere? To not know if you'll make it home?
SKIPPER	Into something rich and strange,
SHONA	Dreaming I'd meet him again. He'd been washed ashore maybe, living an adventure.
SKIPPER	Sea-nymphs hourly ring his knell:
SHONA	The truth hurts too much.
SKIPPER	Ding-dong,
SHONA	Make up wee stories, white lies, imaginary circumstances. Create a fantasy or picture the truth –
SKIPPER	Hark!
SHONA	– a rotting body at the bottom of an empty sea.
SKIPPER	Now I hear them –

SHONA	I wanted to remember.
	See his face, hear his voice.
SKIPPER	Ding-dong, bell.
SHONA	An underwater land.
	An island adventure.
	That was easier.

I dreamed. And I had nightmares. Dreams
and nightmares.
But no facts.

No facts and no memories.

SCENE 14

There is a memorial service, led by the MATE as minister.

The CHORUS enter dressed in black. They sing:

WILL YOUR ANCHOR HOLD.

Will your anchor hold in the storms of life,
When the clouds unfold their wings of strife?
When the strong tides lift, and the cables strain,
Will your anchor drift or firm remain?

We have an anchor that keeps the soul
Steadfast and sure while the billows roll,
Fastened to the Rock which cannot move,
Grounded firm and deep in the Savior's love

*EVE enters; she has aged. There is a distance between her and
SHONA.*

EVE There was a knock on the door. I answered
it and this man from the Mission was there.
And he goes:

SKIPPER commences the role of the Mission representative.

SKIPPER	Can I speak to you?
EVE	And I said tae him, aye, and he says… he says:
SKIPPER	Is there somewhere we can go?
EVE	So we went inside. And he turned and says:
SKIPPER	I'm really sorry ma dear.
	He's gone.
EVE	Aye, he's at the sea.

A beat.

SKIPPER	No. I'm sorry. He's gone.
EVE	*(To SHONA.)* And I'm thinking, whit does he mean, he's *gone*? Then he says there were things he needed to discuss.

Everythin after is a blur. I was in the house and somebody must've gotten you from school, taken you home.

I remember tryin tae be fine and tellin you everythin wis gan tae be okay. And there wis folk in the house and all I wanted to do was just go away. Masel. I still wisna believing that he was… I couldn't take it in that he wisna comin back.

A beat.

Then they were saying something about a body and gasses. A body will come up then go back down and then it'll come back up and if they dinna get it the first time then they can get it the second time and then it'll sink again and… that's it. Part of me wanted them

tae find one and part of me didna because
I thought he'd still come walking back in.
But then the boat came back and everybody
else was back and he wasn't... then I was
hoping they'd get the body so we could have
a funeral. Then the Mission man was saying,
right, you can have a memorial service.

The service... walking into the kirk and
seeing a sea of black. That's it.

EVE looks over to the CHORUS.

One day you're a family and the next...
it's gone. All gone. You've got your future
mapped out. Then somebody comes,
there's a knock at the door and that's
it – everything. Your hopes, your dreams
– gone. I mind sitting down at night and
thinkin: what am'aa goin tae do? What
am'aa goin tae do? I've got a bairn. What
am'aa goin tae do? I had no idea. And then
during the day, I was playing mam, still
like... we'll do this and we'll do that... then
I'd go to my bed and put the pillow over my
head and cry.

A beat.

Then the nightmares started. The same one
over and over – I came in about from my
work and I walked in the door and thought,
there's somebody in the house. And Jock
would come out the shower wearing a
towel and he'd say: '*hello, you're there! What
have you done with ma clothes?*' And I would
say... we had a service. We had a memorial
service! I didna ken you were coming back

73

and they said that you were... and then
I'd wake up in the middle of the night
sweating. In tears. I had that nightmare for
years. I could see him... and then it would
fade. He would fade away.

The worst thing is I never got to say
goodbye. I mean, I canna mind the last
thing I said to him before he went to sea.
I canna mind...

SKIPPER places a hand on her shoulder.

A memory.

We'd been arguing. About the boat. The
life. I didn't want it. And then... he was
gone. Every fight plays through your head,
over and over. Whit you should have said.
Whit you shouldn't have. The bits you can't
remember. Did I tell him I loved him? Did I
tell him he meant the world to me?

I pray I did. I pray that he knew.

SHONA approaches EVE.

SHONA	Mum?
EVE	I've told you everythin I know.
SHONA	You never really found out what happened.
EVE	He went over the side. That's it.
SHONA	But the inquiry?
EVE	The men went but nobody spoke about it.
SHONA	What about Kevin?

EVE	He widna speak a word. He won't tell you anything. He hasna spoken to me for near twenty years.
SHONA	Why?
EVE	I never really belonged in that world.

A beat.

SHONA	Somebody must know something.
EVE	Please Shona. Leave it be.
SHONA	I'll find out, Mum. I have to.
EVE	Let the deceased live in peace.
SHONA	I don't understand. Doesn't it drive you crazy? Not knowing?
EVE	He made me promise, Shona. He told me to move on if anything happened. I did. I did because I had to.
SHONA	He wasn't here to tell me the same.

A beat.

EVE	You're asking all these questions. Asking people tae talk. Maybe you'll hear stories. But that's all they are. Stories.
	He's gone. Nothing will change that.
SHONA	I need your blessing, Mum. I need you know that you're okay with me doing this.
EVE	Whatever you're trying tae do, whitever you're searchin for… he's never coming back.
SHONA	It'll bring him back to me.

EVE   Then I hope you find whit you're lookin for.

A beat.

SHONA   I will. I have to.

EVE hugs her daughter. She rejoins the CHORUS.

                  She's moved on. They've all moved on. It's
                  just me.

SKIPPER   Trapped in time. The space between.

SHONA   It'll bring him back to me.

SCENE 15

SHONA is with the CHORUS.

SHONA   I've got to talk to Kevin.

SKIPPER   A skipper never tells.

SHONA   He was in charge? That day?

SKIPPER   Aye. The chief o the clan, the heid o the table.

SHONA   Then he must know something.

SKIPPER points to the CHORUS.

SKIPPER   Talk tae them first.
                  Best tae ken the tide afore ye set sail.

VOICES   4. See. Ye put yer life in a skipper's hands.
                  Aye – literally.

The sound of the shipping forecast.

                  1. Ye'd be sitting wi twa, three skippers and
                  the forecast comes in: North, North-West,
                  severe storm gale eight to ten, storm force at
                  times… and ane of them wid say:

SKIPPER	Och, ye'll nae get that wind, that wind's by. We'll just let her go, boys.
VOICES	1. You've waited for the forecast and they didna believe it!

2. If you're the skipper you've got that much mare tae think aboot… my wife would say to me the night afore I left:

5. "You're at the sea noo, aren't you?"

2. She'd be speakin awa and gettin nae answer.

5. "You're at the sea noo."

3. INS – the Inverness registration. Ken fit that stands for?

2. I Never Stop.

3. I Never Sleep.

2. Same difference.

1. I remember this one time the crew were knackered – the deck was full of fish and… weel, ye canna leave fish oot for too long on the deck. So I says, look guys, go awa tae your beds for four hours and I'll keep a watch. So I waited two ooers then I went down and shifted all the clocks forward. And then I shouted them up – right loons! So aabody gets oot their beds like spring lambs thinkin they've had four hours sleep. They only had two! Some folk wid probably say:

4. You coorse bastard!

1. But, ken, it's on your heid if the crew come hame wi a pay or not. You've got six, seven men dependin on you.

3. This one skipper… he locked us ootside for twa days workin wi the fish on the deck. Locked the door on us. Never even got a cup o tea or nothin.

4. Nae allowed back in, maybe twenty ooers stuck oot there, nae a bite tae eat.

3. That boy wis a tyrant.

2. The skippers on these boats wis like a God.

3. Aye, they didna put up wi ony shite.

1. Complete dictatorship.

2. Anybody that didn't do exactly whit they said were told –

3. Fuck you! Fucking, if you're nae fucking happy then you can fucking go.

1. They were under a lot of pressure.

4. Or they put themselves under a lot of pressure.

2. That pressure affected aa o us.

1. Three guys buy a million pound boat, that's whit some of them cost tae build, you ken? Same as buying a hoose – ye'v got tae meet the mortgage payment every month.

2. They'd dee onythin tae get money. So if that meant –

3. Longer hours.

	4. Longer trips.
	1. Dumping fish.
	2. Aye… if that was the best financial way forward – weel, they were gan tae dee it. All o it.
SKIPPER	They werena aa like that, mind. You got the odd ane that wis really good.
SHONA	And what about Kevin? Was he one of the good ones?

No response.

SCENE 16

KATH and KEVIN's house. SHONA and SKIPPER watch.

KEVIN	Denner ready?
KATH	Nearly.

They kiss. She notices he is holding something behind his back.

	Whit ye hiding?

She reaches for it.

KEVIN	Nothin.
KATH	Have ye got me a wee pressie?
KEVIN	Maybe.
KATH	Show me.
KEVIN	Whit's it worth?
KATH	I'm nae gan tae beg you for it.
KEVIN	I wis only jokin. Here, tak it.

It's a small box with a necklace inside.

KATH	Thank you. It's lovely.
KEVIN	You dinna seem best impressed.
KATH	Och, I love it. I do.

A beat.

	It's jeest…
KEVIN	Whit?
KATH	Aa the time that you and Jock spoke aboot gettin yer ain boat –
KEVIN	Where's this gan?
KATH	Look, I'm jeest saying, aa the time that you spoke aboot it, Eve wid go on aboot how we'd get tae see you mare, how you'd go back tae the West Coast.
KEVIN	And whit?
KATH	I understaun whit she meant.
KEVIN	Meanin?
KATH	Ye got yer ain boat. You've made a fortune. But whit's it worth, Kev?
KEVIN	Whit the hell is that supposed tae mean?
KATH	I never get tae see you.
KEVIN	For fucks sake –
KATH	You're makin aa this money an we dinna get tae go oot an enjoy it. A nicht in the pub if ye'r hame for two days.

KEVIN	You widna hae this hoose if it wisna for whit I wis dein. Ye widna hae yer fancy clase an yer jewellery if I wisna dein whit I wis dein.
	Aa *you* need tae dee is sit at hame, keep the hoose tidy, mak a meal when I'm back – an ye'r moanin aboot it?
KATH	I'm nae moanin, Kev. Weel, I am, but –
KEVIN	Aye, you are.
KATH	Wid ye nae think aboot gan back tae the West noo?
KEVIN	Christ, it's ma ain fuckin brother comin back tae haunt me.

A look to SHONA.

A pause.

KATH	That wis unnecessary.
KEVIN	Aa he used tae bang on aboot, him and Eve, and noo you. Christ, can you nae just shut up and accept whit I've made for this femily?
KATH	Aye, you've made us rich. But we're nae a family.

KEVIN exits but KATH stays.

SHONA	What happened to them?
SKIPPER	He got his ain boat. Got a licence. Started gan oot even longer trips.

KATH turns to SHONA and says:

KATH   I used tae think he wis dein it for his
            brother. Used tae think he wis oot there
            trying tae build the business they could've
            had together. Maybe he wis for a start.
            Maybe he just forgot whit he wis dein oot
            there in the first place. Because I never
            heard Jock's name again. I only ever heard
            aboot the money.

SHONA   I don't understand where this is going.

SKIPPER   *(To SHONA.)* Halcyon days are on the
            horizon, lass. Time is the faither of truth.

SCENE 17

*The CHORUS circle SHONA telling their versions of what happened
to JOCK.*

VOICES   1. The story I heard wis that they pit a net
            ower the side, he went ower wi it, got hurt
            and couldna get back aboard.

            5. I thought somebody went oot ower the
            side tae try tae get him?

            3. Aye, it's nae as if he jeest disappeared.

            2. The boat they were workin on wis higher
            oot the water – nae designed for gettin fowk
            back.

            4. They couldna get him oot the water. Two
            of you couldna pull a lad up on ane of those
            boats. You couldna.

            6. He must've got hurt on the way ower.

SHONA   He was hurt?

VOICES	1. That's the only logical reason for him nae bein able tae help himsel.
	2. Bang on the heid?
	1. That's aa you need. That's fit must've happened.
	4. We dinna wear hard hats, ye see?
	5. Och, no! He wis drooned, whit else can ye say? They tried to save him and they never managed. Terrible.
	1. See, I think he wis in the water and the water's aas cold. It wid numb aathin.
	2. He went oot ower the side. He wis swept away. That's whit happened.
	3. He just hadna tae be. It wis his time, a hell of a thing that, but it wis his time.
SKIPPER	You'll never win wi the sea.
VOICES	2. Fit's for ye will nae go by ye… if it's meant to be, it'll be.
	5. If it's there for you, that's your fate. It's hellish. But that's the way I look at it.
	7. It wis his time.
	6. Maybe he tired himsel oot and they couldna get him up quick enough.
	3. He wis one of the best sweemers that I ever seen. Ken, really, he wis.
	1. It wisna anythin tae dee wi sweemin! I'm a nae bad swimmer but… it's nae a case of swimmin. It's a case of survivin. Ken?

4. Tryin tae keep yersel afloat.

2. Conserve yer energy.

3. That's fit the aul fishermen wid say.

1. There wis 30ft waves. See? 30ft waves. That's a hell o a watter for a wee boatie.

2. It wisna that bad weather when it happened!

4. Aye, there wis a storm.

2. No there wisna! A wee drap rain.

1. To my opinion, there wis a lot of mistakes with the crew of that boat and where does the mistake start wi a crew? It starts fae the skipper doon.

2. Aye, blame the skipper.

3. Nah, blame the crew.

1. The weather!

4. The boat!

1. There had tae be mistakes there somewhere. Agreed?

ALL	Aye. Mistakes.
SHONA	Mistakes?
SKIPPER	Mistakes.
VOICE	2. An accident!
ALL	An accident.
SHONA	An accident?
SKIPPER	An accident.

VOICES	4. It wisna weather.
	5. Maybe it wis weather.
SHONA	Weather or not weather… what's the truth? Please.
SKIPPER	The truth…?
VOICE	2. The truth never came oot, I think. To be honest… I think there wis a lot covered up.
SHONA	What was covered up?
VOICE	1. Look, you canna beat that fuckin great big sea, ken?
SHONA	WHAT was covered up?
VOICE	3. Nothin wis covered up! Dinna be stupid.
SKIPPER	An accident… a mistake… a cover-up…
SHONA	What is this? None of them know! None of them are telling me anything. Bits of this, bits of that but nothing. Nothing!
SKIPPER	Maybe they dinna want ye tae get hurt.
SHONA	I'm getting hurt by not knowing anything! The police, the courts, the coast guards, the village – nobody knows! Why? What's the big secret that no-one will talk about?
SKIPPER	Fit if there is no big secret? Maybe naebody kens an that's the end o it.
SHONA	But it's not the end, is it? Not for me.
	(To the CHORUS.) Please. Help me. Tell me!

The CHORUS exit.

Stop. Come back. Come back!

(To SKIPPER.) Why are they leaving?

SKIPPER   We aa move on eventually.

SHONA sees MEG and BILLY in the CHORUS.

SHONA   *(To MEG.)* You must know, you must
                 remember something. Gran, please. Tell me
                 what you know.

MEG   It wis a long time ago.

SHONA   But –

MEG   Shona. No buts. Please. Ye need to leave
                 whit happened in the past.

SHONA   I don't know which is which now.

SKIPPER   Their past, your future. Ye'r askin them to
                 relive it. Aa o them.

SKIPPER gestures to MEG.

MEG   *(To SHONA.)* Billy didna live long efter Jock
                 wis lost.
                 The shock o it, I think.
                 He'd followed his faither tae the sea.
                 Billy maybe blamed himsel for that.
                 But that's jeest whit happened in those days.

A moment.

BILLY   *(To MEG.)* I keep expectin him tae walk
                 through the door.

SKIPPER   *(To SHONA.)* They lost a son.

MEG   I want tae move, Billy.

SKIPPER   It tore the femily apairt.

BILLY	We canna, Meg. Far wid we go?
MEG	I canna look at it anymore. I canna hear it aa the time. I hate the sea, I hate it.
BILLY	She wis good to us.
MEG	My hale life has revolved aroon it. Everythin has been aboot that monster oot there. Whit's it gein us? Really? Whit has it ever done for us?
BILLY	It's been everythin. It's been oor life. We canna leave.
MEG	It took my ain dad. Ma son. Kevin's changed. You're the only ane it left me wi. It's taken everythin. I canna bear tae look at it anymore.
BILLY	We'll get by, Meg. We ayways do.
MEG	Nae this time.
BILLY	You canna blame the sea. We chose this life.
MEG	I didna.
BILLY	You canna think that wye. Jock widna have wanted it. He loved the sea, ye ken that. He loved it.
MEG	Did he? Or wis he just as disillusioned as the rest o us? I canna dee it onymare. I'm sorry Billy, nae this time.
BILLY	Ye'r gan tae have tae. You've got the bairns, ye'v got Eve.
MEG	No.

BILLY	Yes. Nae mare. He's gone. There's nothin we can dee aboot it. Ye'r gan tae have to pull yersel thegither an get on wi it. He's nae the first an he winna be the last.
MEG	Dinna be so cold.
BILLY	He was my son too.
MEG	It winna be the same. Nae this time.

SKIPPER gestures to BILLY.

BILLY	On oor anniversary, we were meant tae go tae Shetland. Kevin got us tickets an she didna want tae go on the ferry in case she wid cross ower where he wis lost. Thinkin… it must've been hellish. Crossin on the ferry. Cos he was never found and… and that's the bit. That's the bit. She wis niver the same efter he wis lost. Maybe it took one too many fae her.

There wis a body meant to be found at the back shore and she says: |
MEG	That's Jock home.
BILLY	A mither, you see? A mither.
MEG	That's Jock, that's him comin hame.
BILLY	Jeest onythin tae think… And it wisna him. It wisna.

I used tae stand at that windae and greet – far are ye? Aye, mony a time, where are ye, Jock? I'd stand an look at the sea. Ay looked at the sea – a fisherman. I've thought I heard him shoutin once. Just the imagination. |
| MEG | He wis niver the same efter Jock was lost. |

BILLY	She wis niver the same.

A beat.

MEG	Then nae long efter…

BILLY exits.

Bilbo Billy. Thief o the sea.
He wis never really content on the land.

A beat.

Aye. I lost Jock. But I lost my man an'aa.

MEG exits.

SKIPPER	*(To SHONA.)* How do ye live with the dead? A mither and faither. D'ye understand? They aa weathered the storm.
SHONA	And Kevin? What did he do?
SKIPPER	Fishes live in the sea, as men do a-land; the great ones eat up the little ones.
SHONA	Always talking riddles.
SKIPPER	I telt ye, quine. We'll tell your story – if you listen tae oors. There's a storm comin.

SCENE 18

KATH and KEVIN's house.

EVE is visiting KATH. SHONA and SKIPPER watch.

EVE	Thanks again for havin me round.
KATH	You dinna need tae thank me. I hivna seen ye in yonks. I wanted tae hae ye roon for denner last time Kev wis back but he wis that busy and… y'ken…

| EVE | Aye, I ken. |

EVE looks around at her surroundings.

	I guess he's dein well.
KATH	Aye, he's deen weel.
EVE	And you're lookin great.
KATH	Thank you. I got masel ane o those exercise bikes. Wi the kids gettin on, I had a bit mare time, ye ken? Thocht I should try and dee somethin wi masel. Nae gettin ony younger!

A beat.

	I'm sorry... I dinna ken whit tae...
EVE	I ken. No, dinna worry. I ken. It's life, Kath. I'm happy for you.
KATH	How's the bairn?
EVE	Och, she's fine. She's desperate to go see some show – she's aa into books and stories – but the prices... I'm determined tae find a way but...
KATH	I could – (help)
EVE	No.
KATH	But – (I could help)
EVE	No. It's not your place. I'm dein alright.
KATH	But ye'r workin flat oot. I hivna seen ye for months because ye'r either workin or ye'r studyin or ye'r runnin the bairn aroon. I dinna ken how you dee it.
EVE	I dee it because I have tae.

KATH	You hivna thocht o maybe lookin for anither man?
EVE	Kath.
KATH	I dinna mean any wrong by it. But you, ken, it's been a few years noo. Naebody would think onythin o it. You're still young enough, ye could start again.
EVE	No. I ken you dinna mean any harm. But no. Nae when the bairn's still young. If I meet someone in the future.... maybe. But nae noo. I've got to get her to the big school, on her way, maybe university and then I'll have done what Jock wanted.
KATH	You're a good person.
EVE	No. I'm a bitter person. But I try nae to let it eat me.
KATH	Are ye bitter aboot Kevin?

A beat.

	I shouldna have said that.
EVE	I canna change whit happened. I canna think like that.
KATH	I do. I miss him, y'ken. I miss him a lot. They'll never be anither laugh like Jock's. He wis a good man.
EVE	Shona will never ken it.
KATH	We'll tell her.

KATH looks at SHONA.

One day, we'll tell her everythin.

A pause.

EVE	Kath.
KATH	Aye?
EVE	I'm leaving.
KATH	Whit?
EVE	I'm moving tae Aberdeen.

A beat.

There's nothin here for me anymore.

KATH	I'm here. Kevin's – (here)
EVE	I have to do this. Everything's just a reminder of whit could've been. I've got to take the bairn and move on.
KATH	Whit aboot Meg? Losin the bairn… she'd be devastated.
EVE	You've got each other. This is your life… it was never really mine. Please… please don't be angry with me.

I jeest – canna do it anymore.

A beat.

KATH	I think the same sometimes.
EVE	But you and Kev, you're … this is where you belong. Your home.
KATH	Maybe. Och. Sometimes yer mind wanders, ken? Ye think o other places. Other lives.

But whit else wid Kevin dee? He's torn that ocean apart, I canna imagine him turnin his

92

	back on it noo. It's aa I ever hear aboot – quotas this and quotas that. Black landings. It doesna change. He thinks they're takin whit's rightfully theirs. The sea's a free zone, who can tell them tae stop?
	I asked him tae leave. Telt him he's made enough money tae dee us for a lifetime. But he winna. Canna stay awa. Salt in his veins.
EVE	Whit did they use tae say? You and me –
KATH	– versus the sea.

A moment.

EVE	I miss the fish. The frys he'd bring home.
KATH	Ye ken, I've ay cooked the fish at hame.
EVE	Aye, I mind you saying that.
KATH	Funny, isn't it? You'd think they'd be the big experts but, nope, they haun it ower an let ye get on wi it.
EVE	Jock would fry them in our hoose. He wis good at fryin fish.
KATH	Mmm, see a fried fish? Nothin tastes better.
EVE	You'll mak me hungry!
KATH	And see a bitty fish done in batter... ahhh. Billy wis the best ane at dein the fish in batter. Mind that? Wowee. And the batter wid puff up. Oh. It wid just melt in yer... oooh. Absolutely delicious. Jeest so, so good.
EVE	I dinna think there's a fish I dinna like. I never thought I'd be like that afore I met

	Jock but… och, love everything. Sardines tae halibut. Lemon sole –
KATH	Lemon sole!
EVE	– plaice, haddock…. I love a haddock. You'll nae beat that. Know what else I love? Your cullen skink.
KATH	Ma cullen skink. I jeest adore it. I'll mak that next time ye'r roon.
EVE	Aye. Next time.

A pause.

	I don't really eat it anymore. The prices they charge in the shops.
KATH	Let me get you a baggie o whites afore ye go. I've got plenty in the freezer.
EVE	You dinna need to do that.
KATH	How nae? Half my fry wid dee me a fortnicht!
	Ye'r still family, Eve. Dinna forget it.
EVE	Thank you. That's affa kind.
KATH	I'm yer pal. I'm femily. It's whit we're supposed tae dee.
	I'll ay help you an the bairn. Anythin I can dee for you or Shona, now or later, wherever ye end up… I will. I promise.

EVE exits but KATH remains.

SKIPPER	*(To SHONA.)* There's your washed up remains, yer aftermath o the storm.
SHONA	There's only Kevin left.

SKIPPER	He'll maybe nae meet, he'll maybe nae tell.
SHONA	He might.
SKIPPER	What happens at the sea –
SHONA	He's the last one. The last chance.
SKIPPER	So it's time tae face yer present? Tak the lay o the land.
SHONA	I'm ready.

SHONA approaches KATH.

> Will you ask him to talk to me? Ask him to meet?

A beat.

KATH	Aye, quine. I will.

They hug.

A low rumble of thunder.

SKIPPER	Whistle the wind
	Through the darkened night,
	Align time an tide
	And they will unite.
	Let the tempest swell
	An the black horse roar,
	Tae the eye of the storm
	The blood an the core.

A light shines through the darkness.

SCENE 19

SKIPPER sits back on the perch; ready, observing.

A single spotlight. A sparse table and two chairs. KEVIN sits in one, arms folded. SHONA sits opposite.

She is flustered. She struggles to take off her jacket then rakes through her bag pulling out a notebook, pens and a diary. Finally, she retrieves a dictaphone which she places squarely on the table. She presses the record button.

A breath.

SHONA   Okay.

    A beat.

KEVIN   Ye'r a journalist.

SHONA   I was.

KEVIN   Is this gan tae be in the paper?

SHONA   This? About my dad?

              No. This is for me.

KEVIN   Why the dictaphone?

SHONA   To remember.

    A beat.

KEVIN   Whit do ye want from me?

SHONA   The truth.

    A pause.

              I need to know what happened.

KEVIN   Trying to find someone tae blame?

SHONA	I want answers.
KEVIN	You should call the MAIB.
SHONA	I did. I tried everywhere. You're the last one.
KEVIN	It wis a long time ago.
SHONA	You could never forget a night like that.
KEVIN	Whit happens at the sea – (stays at the sea)
SHONA	Not this time.
KEVIN	Maybe ye shouldna be stickin yer nose in.
SHONA	Is that really what you think?
KEVIN	Fowk dinna like journalists.
SHONA	I'm your niece. Your brother's daughter. And I'm probably the closest thing you've got left to him.

KEVIN doesn't respond.

I don't know what I expected but it sure as hell wasn't that you'd treat me like – a journalist.

A beat.

I've spent my whole life wondering who he was. And now I'm borrowing everyone else's stories, piecing together all these fragments… but you're the only person left who can actually tell me what happened.

Still no response. SHONA stands and starts to pack up her belongings.

This is a waste of time.

KEVIN   Ye look like him.

A moment.

               Got that same big, sad een.

SHONA   Are you going to talk to me?

KEVIN   It wis the wrong brother. Did naebody tell
               ye that? Aabody thocht it. He wis the good
               ane. Ay the blue-eyed boy, the ane who pit
               his mither afore onybody... his wife, his kid.

               You.

SHONA   All I know is that I was a little girl, waiting
               for my dad to get back – I don't know how
               long I waited, sat by the window, looking
               out. Day after day. I just know that he never
               came home.

KEVIN   Ye were too young tae understaun.

SHONA   But I'm not now.

               I want a piece of him that's mine.
               Something, anything, to hold onto. I'll never
               have memories, I've accepted that. But I
               thought, at least, I could have the facts. The
               truth.

KEVIN   See, you want some sort o clear-cut
               explanation – but it disna work like that.

SHONA   Please. Just tell me what you remember.
               That's all I want.

A hesitation.

KEVIN   There's naethin... definite when ye'r at the
               sea. Everythin happens sae quick when ye'r

98

oot there. Time sorta… ye canna see much. Canna hear much. It's jeest adrenaline. Throw the dice, the game starts… and ye play tae win. Russian roulette.

The sound and sight of the sea.

A moment in time.

I mind the wind wis howlin and we wis blawin aa ower the place.

I wis in the wheelhoose and I could hear some sort o commotion. Maybe they shouted me tae come oot. The crew were tryin tae haul the nets and they were dein it manually cos they'd got stuck in the propeller. I think I wis standin aboot here and Jock wis maybe there and – are you alright with this?

SHONA   It's what I've been waiting for.

KEVIN   I think he wis standin on the net. Aye. If he'd been staunin on the net then, when they got pulled ower the rail, that'd be the wye he geen ower the side.

It aa happened that fast, I dinna ken exactly whit went on. But tae this day, I blame the wellies. That's whit I telt the inquiry. We were aa gettin these new welly boots, ken? He'd on a new pair of these boots and they'd a great thick tread and maybe the tread got caught in the net because he jeest… sort o went head first ower the rail. And then… panic.

I mind we threw a rope but he couldna hing ontae it… and aince ye'r in the watter, ye'r speakin aboot minutes, ken? Because the hypothermia, you get weaker and weaker. We tried tae get him back and tried tae get him back. Nothin wis workin. And then… in the end, I think he jeest succumbed tae the hypothermia.

If we'd got him back in the first minute, he'd maybe have been aaright.

A pause.

SHONA   You blame the welly boots.

KEVIN   Ye dinna train for gettin fowk back, ken? Us fishermen… we dinna train for it.

A beat.

I'm sorry.

SHONA stands.

I said I'm sorry.

A moment.

SCENE 20

The CHORUS surround the stage. SKIPPER steps forward into the present.

SHONA   What are you doing?

SKIPPER   Ye said ye'd listen. It's time.

SHONA   But he's told me the story.

SKIPPER   Your story. Nae mine.

SHONA steps back and SKIPPER takes her place, staring at KEVIN intently.

KEVIN   Whit you lookin at?

SKIPPER   Ah, ye can see me noo, can ye? Why wid
                 that be, eh Kev boy?

KEVIN   Whit are you supposed tae be? Ma fuckin
                 conscience?

SKIPPER   Have ye got ane o them? Weel...

SKIPPER 'doffs their cap'.

KEVIN   Look. I telt her everythin I could, everythin
                 I could remember.

SKIPPER   Ye didna tell her aboot yer licence, did ye?

KEVIN   Whit's that got tae dee wi onythin?

SKIPPER   That ye sold yer boat but kept yer licence.

KEVIN   That's got fuck all tae dee with Jock.

SKIPPER   Aye. One loss is a tragedy. Hoo much blood
                 have ye got on yer hands noo?

KEVIN   I'm nae even at the sea onymare.

SKIPPER   Bullseye. Aye, she kens ye'r a *Slipper skipper.*

VOICES   *(Whispered.) Slipper skipper. Slipper skipper.*

KEVIN   Has she been speakin tae my wife? Is that
                 whit's gan on? Kath's been moothin off?

SKIPPER   Doesna metter. She kens that you sit on yer
                 erse aa day whilst loons are oot there riskin
                 their lives. And you're makin mare money
                 than they'll ever hae, cooried doon in yer
                 hoose wi yer paper fish.

101

KEVIN	I'm nae harmin anyone. She canna judge me.
SKIPPER	But I can.
VOICES	We can.
KEVIN	Get tae fuck.
SKIPPER	That fleet doon at the herbour should've been replaced long ago. Six million a boat. The young loons hivna got that money. Because far's their earnings gan? Tae you.
KEVIN	Bullshit. I *help* them. When they canna land whit they've caught, I'm the one they call.
SKIPPER	Is that fit ye caw it? Help? Chargin them a fortune tae lease a wee bit o yer quota?
KEVIN	Aye. Stops them fae dumpin the fish anyroad.
SKIPPER	Chargin them mare per box than they'll ever mak on the market jeest so they can land a hard day's catch.
KEVIN	I didna design the system. I didna mak the rules.
SKIPPER	But ye ken how tae play the game.
KEVIN	I'm nae dein onythin wrong.
SKIPPER	Legally ye'r nae. But dee ye think it's fair?
KEVIN	Naebody ever got anywhere by bein fair.
SKIPPER	Fit next, then? Go on. Ye'r gan tae sell the license?
KEVIN	Aye.
SKIPPER	Sell it for mare money.

KEVIN	Exactly whit I'm entitled tae.
SKIPPER	And fa will ye sell it tae?
KEVIN	Fa do ye think? The highest bidder.
SKIPPER	Why don't ye give it back tae the village?
KEVIN	Whit the hell are ye on aboot?
SKIPPER	Gee it back tae them. The loons. Gee them a chance.
KEVIN	Ye'r haverin. Talkin shite.
SKIPPER	You got it for nothin.
KEVIN	Aye – and noo it's ma pension.
SKIPPER	Ye winna need that mony millions.
KEVIN	I can sell ma licence tae faever I want.
SKIPPER	Ye cry oot aboot protectin yer watters but ye'd sell them in a heartbeat.
KEVIN	At least I'd be in control o it.
SKIPPER	And fa will ye sell tae? The Dutch? The French?
KEVIN	Maybe.
SKIPPER	Tae a Supermarket?
KEVIN	If they had the highest bid.

SHONA stands.

SHONA	To a supermarket? Is that possible?
SKIPPER	You'd sell yer ain waters.
KEVIN	My licence.

SKIPPER	Their waters. Oor waters.
	Loons oot there nicht an day fechtin the ocean, fightin for their lives as you dee fuck all. Playing God wi a wee bit o paper. Hoo mony loons have been lost tryin tae make a living? How mony have died under your watch?
KEVIN	It's my right tae reap a reward. I gave ma life tae that sea.
SKIPPER	No. You didna. Yer brother did. You jeest scraped up fitever wis left.
KEVIN	The sea wis raped a long time afore I came along.
SKIPPER	Oh aye, that she wis. But you personally fucked her corpse.

A pause.

KEVIN	Ye'r not even real.
SKIPPER	Then whose voice can ye hear? Grating awa in yer heid?
KEVIN	I dinna hae tae listen tae this shite.

KEVIN exits. SKIPPER calls after him.

SKIPPER	It'll tak mare whisky than even you can afford tae droon me oot.

SKIPPER summons the CHORUS.

And here, in the now, we bear witness and stand in judgement. The spirit, the watter and the blood.

SKIPPER points to SHONA.

Your story is hers and hers is yours. It's aa bound thegither.

(To SHONA.) This is my present. You think on it. The untold war o man versus the elements.

Go. Write the story. There's my truth.

SCENE 21

SKIPPER is with the CHORUS. They sing:

ETERNAL FATHER

Eternal Father, strong to save
Whose arm hath bound the restless wave
Who biddest the mighty ocean deep
Its own appointed limits keep
Oh, hear us when we cry to Thee
For those in peril on the sea.

O Trinity of love and power
Our family shield in danger's hour
From rock and tempest, fire and foe
Protect us wheresoever we go
Thus evermore shall rise to Thee
Glad hymns of praise from land and sea

VOICE   2. When you look back, it was a wasted life.

ALL   Niver.

VOICES   2. A wasted life.

               1. Never went tae the fishing for money, ye only went for a laugh.

               2. Any money ye made was invested tae the public house.

               4. That's when fishin was fun.

105

1. The first thing boys ask noo is – have ye got Sky TV aboard?

2. Dumpin at that scale. A travesty o justice.

4. The fish are still deid – they canna go ower the side and jeest sweem awa.

1. We were takin in 60 boxes a day o white uns. Gutted, boxed, iced. Came in and there wis a lorry on the pier, 40 gallon drums on it. Aa for feedin seals.

2. Just thought naethin o it – awa back oot and catch mare.

3. Naebody in the world would dee whit we were dein.

1. When I think back noo I think, fuckin hell, nae bloody wonder there's nae fish in the sea.

2. The seals ate them all.

SCENE 22

SHONA and SKIPPER. The CHORUS are all present.

SHONA   This is for you.

SHONA holds out a newspaper. SKIPPER takes it and reads the headline.

SKIPPER   'Slipper skipper's sell out'.

               From front page tae fish wrap.

SHONA   I don't have much influence but... maybe someone will listen.

A moment.

SKIPPER	Yer voyage is over.
SHONA	It'll never be over. I don't even know what's real.
SKIPPER	Aabody's truth is their ain.

SHONA sees JOCK in the CHORUS. There is a distance between them.

SHONA	*(To JOCK.)* I'm sorry if I didn't find yours.
SKIPPER	Fit happens at the sea –
SHONA	– stays at the sea.
SKIPPER	I'm sorry.
SHONA	I'm not. It brought him back. For me.
SKIPPER	We learn by the past, live wi oor present, hope fer the future.
	We'll niver ken the worth o watter til the well is dry.
SHONA	*(To JOCK.)* They maybe don't remember you. But I do.

The sound of the wind and the sea.

The CHORUS stand to remember the men and boats lost at sea.

VOICES	Donnie Young, 43, lost from the "Ardent II", 1989.
	James Bruce, 49, lost from the "Sparkling Star", 1999
	Alexander P Mair, 30, lost from the "Trident" 1974
	Ian C Innes, 25, lost from the "Margarita", 1979

James P Pratt, 32,
lost from the "Mayflower", 1972

The "Premier", 1990:
John Alexander Edwards, 36
Joseph 'Joe' Edwards, 31
Neil Edwards, 24
Sandy Main, 26
William 'Billy' Main, 33
John Davidson Ross, 46

The "Acacia Wood", 1978
Andrew Cadger, 21
Alexander Jack, 29
Alexander Jack Snr, 57
James Jack, 29
Peter McKenzie, 32
David McLennan, 37
David Morrison, 25
Paul Stewart, 21
William Stewart, 25

Peter Cowie, 45,
lost from the "Ann Wood", 1976

William Alexander Findlay, 35,
the "Ann Wood", 1982

James A Phimister, 34,
the "Morning Dawn", 1984

James Alexander, 44,
the "Clarkwood", 1973

Peter Buchan, 35, the "Crimond", 1970

John Crawford, 35
Alexander Davidson, 27
Robert McKenzie, 23

William 'Billy' McKenzie, 30
Alexander 'Sandy' McKenzie, 32
Brian Peterkin, 23
David R J Robertson, 19
All lost with the "Rosebud", 1980

Lewis Stewart Smith, 42
Alexander Reid Flett, 57
Patrick Devine, 27
Edward Wilson, 19
Gordon Stewart, 18
All lost with the "Arcadia", 1983

George Murray, 62, the "Arlanda", 1986

Robert Cowie, 33, the "Begonia", 1980

George Wood, 33, the "Mizpah", 1970

James Murray, 54, the "Ben Loyal", 1974

John Clark, 26, the "Heather Sprig", 2006

James Watt, 21, the "Boy Peter", 1970

"Star Divine", 1970 –
Lewis M Stopel, 18 and
John Wood, 56

"Ocean Monarch", 1979 –
John Clark, 31
William Coull, 33
John Alexander Reid, 32
Alan Sutherland, 17
Gordon Taylor, 29
Walter Thain, 37
Barton C Sudding, 23

"Guiding Star", 1974 –
William I Farquhar, 37

and Alexander Thain, 54

"Bounteous", 1980 –
Joseph Bowie, 26
Russell Hillier, 25
Edward R Phimister, 30

John Alexander Bowie, 39,
lost from the "Conquest", 1970

George Cowie, 57,
lost from the "Conquest", 1990

John Bennet Farquhar, 31,
the "Surmount", 1980

George Alex Robertson, 30,
the "Cairngorm", 1982

John Morrison, 61, the "Elma", 1975

Sandy Bruce, 38
Richard Clark, 45
Francis Goodall, 30
William G Grant, 24
John Innes, 45
George Reid, 35
All from the "Celerity", 1981

"Bon Ami", 1985 –
David Lovie, 32
Matthew McFarlane, 38
Chris McInnes, 38
Eric Mitchell, 38
John Sim, 26
Christopher Hunt, 16

John Cowie, 46, the "Flower", 1970

John Addison, 43,
the "Admiral Van Tromp", 1976

Alexander James Johnston, 56,
the "Coral Strand", 1983

Geddes Falconer, 24, the "Odelia", 1975

James Falconer Mair, 41,
the "Fair Isle", 1970

Charles R Cargill, 28
David Flett, 24
Edward G Lawson, 30
James Lobban, 52
Murray Lobban, 21
Richard G Mair, 41
– The "Corinthia", 1979

David Mckenzie, 21,
the "Faithful Again", 1972

Alexander Clark, 39,
the "Helena", 1974

Steven A Lorimer, 30,
the "Loraley", 1981

George Geddes, 54,
the "Alexander Bruce", 1972

Stanley Addison, 42, the "Strathella", 1977

"Glen Shiel", 1973 –
Thomas Farquhar, 55 and
Thomas W West, 58

"Loch Erisort", 1981 –
David 'Bing' Bruce, 22 and
Ian W Smith, 29

"Ocean Harvest", 1985 –
Joseph Innes, 28
Kenneth George Innes, 26
Stuart Taylor, 23
Eric White, 34

William George Geddes, 60,
the "Rising Sea", 1980

Leslie Thain, 34, the "Rose Bloom", 1981

Derek G Walker, 30, the "Strathpeffer", 1978

Joseph McIntosh Gauld, 32,
lost from the "Vigilant", 1980

William Cordiner Thomson, 39,
lost from the "Goodwill", 1984

Dennis D Murray, 48, the "Aeolus", 1995

Neil Sutherland, 39 and
David Davidson, 40 –
both lost from "The Brothers", 2006.

Crash of thunder, a flash of lightning leaving the stage in darkness.

THE END.

GLOSSARY

Aa	All	**Canna**	Can't
Aabody	Everybody	**Caw**	Call
Aaricht /		**Cerried**	Carried
Aaright	Alright	**Cerry**	Carry
Aas	So	**Chap**	Knock
Aathin	Everything	**Cheil**	Man
Aboot	About	**Clase**	Clothes
Affa	Awful /	**Cooried**	Huddled
	Awfully	**Coorse**	Course
Afore	Before		or Coarse
Ain	Own	**Craiter**	Creature
Aince	Once	**Dee**	Do
An'aa	As well	**Deen**	Done
Ane	One	**Deid**	Dead
Anither	Another	**Dein**	Doing
Apairt	Apart	**Denner**	Dinner
Aroon	Around		(meaning
Athoot	Without		lunch)
Aul	Old	**Didna**	Didn't
Auler	Older	**Dinna**	Don't
Awa	Away	**Disna**	Doesn't
Ay /		**Div**	Do
Ayways	Always	**Doon**	Down
Aye	Yes	**Dram**	Drink
Aynoo	Right now	**Drap**	Drop
Baggie	Bag	**Drappies**	Drops
Bairn	Child	**Drooned**	Drowned
Baith	Both	**Dunt**	Bump
Banes	Bones	**Eejit**	Idiot
Bide	Stay	**Een**	Eyes
Blawin	Blowing	**Efter**	After
Bonnie	Pretty	**Efterwards**	Afterwards
Brae	Hill	**Eicht**	Eight
Brak	Break	**Erm**	Arm
Caad	Called	**Erse**	Arse

Fa	Who	**Haun**	Hand
Faither	Father	**Haverin**	To be
Fae	From		indecisive
Far	Where	**Heid**	Head
Faw	Fall	**Herbour**	Harbour
Fawin	Falling	**Himsel**	Himself
Feart	Afraid	**Hing**	Hang
Fecht	Fight	**Hiv**	Have
Fechten	Fighting	**Hivna**	Haven't
Femily	Family	**Honkin**	Stinking
Fer	For	**Hoo**	How
Fit	What	**Hoose**	House
Fitever	Whatever	**Ivery**	Every
Fool	Dirty	**Jeest**	Just
Fortnicht	Fortnight	**Joabbie**	Job
Foushty	Rotting	**Ken**	Know
Fowk	Folk	**Kent**	Knew
Freen	Friend	**Kirk**	Church
Gan	Going	**Lass**	Girl
Gaan	Go on	**Licht**	Light
Gassin	Gossiping	**Loon**	Boy
Gee	Give	**Lug**	Ear
Geed	Gave	**Ma**	My
Geen	Went	**Mak**	Make
Gein	Giving	**Mannie**	Man
Glaik	Stupid	**Mare**	More
	person	**Masel**	Myself
Glaikit	Stupid	**Maste**	Most
Greet	Cry	**Merriet**	Married
Gye	Very	**Metter**	Matter
Hadna	Hadn't	**Min**	Man
Hae	Have	**Mind**	Remember
Haein	Having	**Mither**	Mother
Hale	Whole	**Mony**	Many
Hame	Home	**Moo**	Mouth
Haud	Hold	**Moothin**	Mouthing

Nae	Not / no	**Teeny**	Tiny
Naebody	Nobody	**Telt**	Told
Naethin	Nothing	**Thegither**	Together
Nicht	Night	**Themorn**	Tomorrow
Niver	Never	**Thenight /**	
Noo	Now	**Thenicht**	Tonight
O	Of	**Thocht**	Thought
Ony	Any	**Thon**	Them
Onymare	Anymore	**Toon**	Town
Onyroad /		**Twa**	Two
Onywye	Anyway	**Understaun**	Understand
Onythin	Anything	**Watter**	Water
Ooers	Hours	**Wee**	Little
Oor	Our	**Weel**	Well
Oot	Out	**Weet**	Wet
Oota	Out of	**Wheesht**	Shh
Ower	Over	**Wi**	With
Pal	Friend	**Wid**	Would
Peely-wally	Pale	**Widna**	Wouldn't
Pit	Put	**Windae**	Window
Pyed	Paid	**Winna**	Won't
Quine	Girl	**Wis**	Was
Raveled	Confused	**Wisna**	Was not
Roch	Rough	**Wye**	Way
Roon	Round	**Ye**	You
Sae	So	**Yella**	Yellow
Saft	Soft	**Yer**	Your
Scalders	Jellyfish	**Ye'r**	You're
Seek	Sick	**Ye'v**	You've
Sicht	Sight	**Y'ken**	You know
Spik	Speak		
Staunin	Standing		
Sweem	Swim		
Sweemin	Swimming		
Tae	To		
Tak	Take		

WWW.OBERONBOOKS.COM

Follow us on Twitter @oberonbooks
& Facebook @OberonBooksLondon

9 781786 827555